What Every Law Student Really Needs to Know

WHAT EVERY LAW STUDENT REALLY NEEDS TO KNOW

AN INTRODUCTION TO THE STUDY OF AMERICAN LAW

Fourth Edition

TRACEY E. GEORGE
Vice Provost for Faculty Affairs and Professional Education
Charles B. Cox III and Lucy D. Cox Family Chair in Law and Liberty
Professor of Political Science
Vanderbilt University

SUZANNA SHERRY
Herman O. Loewenstein Chair in Law Emerita
Vanderbilt University

ASPEN PUBLISHING

To contact Customer Service, e-mail customer.service@aspenpublishing.com, call 1-800-950-5259, or mail correspondence to:

Aspen Publishing
Attn: Order Department
1 Wall Street
Burlington, MA 01803

Printed in the United States of America.

1 2 3 4 5 6 7 8 9 0

ISBN 979-8-8941-0001-2

Library of Congress Cataloging-in-Publication Data

About Aspen Publishing

Aspen Publishing is a leading provider of legal educational content and digital learning solutions in the U.S. and around the world. Aspen provides best-in-class solutions through authoritative textbooks, written by renowned authors, and breakthrough products such as Connected eBooks, Connected Quizzing, PracticePerfect, and JD-Next.

The Aspen Casebook Series (famously known among law faculty and students as the "red and black" casebooks) encompasses hundreds of highly regarded textbooks in more than eighty disciplines, from large enrollment courses, such as Torts and Contracts, to emerging electives, like Sustainability and the Law of Policing. Study aids such as *Examples & Explanations* help law students master complex subject matter. Aspen's Paralegal, Criminal Justice, and Business Law series bring our hallmark publishing standards to undergraduate students. JD-Next is an innovative online law school prep course and admissions test that offers a realistic preview of law school, teaches underlying skills for academic success, and assesses applicants' academic readiness for law school.

Aspen Publishing is proud to be a UWorld company

Since 2003, UWorld has been a global leader in developing high-quality learning tools for students preparing for high-stakes exams. With a commitment to excellence, UWorld has helped millions of students in undergraduate, graduate, and professional programs in fields such as medicine, nursing, finance, and law achieve their academic and career goals.

Founded by Chandra S. Pemmasani, M.D., during his medical residency, UWorld began focusing on medical education and has since expanded into various academic fields, including law. In 2020, UWorld launched its Legal vertical, starting with its comprehensive Multistate Bar Exam (MBE®) Question Bank, followed by the acquisition of Themis Bar Review, which integrated resources to provide a complete bar exam preparation experience. In 2024, UWorld expanded its offerings by acquiring Aspen Publishing, enhancing its suite of legal education products.

Today, UWorld offers an unparalleled range of study materials that blend active learning methods with expert content, ensuring students and educators can access the most effective resources. From bar preparation to law school success, UWorld is committed to supporting the next generation of legal professionals. Learn more at uworld.com.

To my father, Dr. Larry George, who inspired me to become a teacher

– T.E.G.

To the teachers who inspired me: Nick Clifford, Murray Dry, Richard Epstein, and Geof Stone

– S.S.

SUMMARY OF CONTENTS

CONTENTS

INTRODUCTION

Picture yourself in your first law school class. After some wandering around, you find the classroom. Students already occupy many of the seats in the tiered rows. Everyone looks nice, if a bit anxious. You slip into an empty chair and pull out your laptop. A few more students lugging massive books trickle in. There is some chattering and a sense of excitement in the room, but mostly everyone is focused on the front of the room or on their books.

The professor walks in and the room falls silent. You know her name is Professor O'Connor—it was printed on your class schedule. She sets down a book like those most of your classmates have on their desks. She unfolds a large piece of paper or pulls up on her laptop screen an image that appears to have small photos and names on it.

Suddenly, you hear your name. The professor is talking to you, asking you a question: "Will you please recite the facts and the holding of *Pierson versus Post*?" Every head in the classroom turns to look at you.

You panic. Your heart begins to race. What are "facts" and "holding"? How are you supposed to know anything about Pierson versus Post before the professor begins lecturing? Did you miss something? You find yourself speechless (perhaps for the first time).

Another student volunteers. You feel relieved—for a moment. But then your classmate begins to talk about "the plaintiff" and "the New York Supreme Court" and other unfamiliar words you don't even catch, as the professor nods approvingly. You can't follow the conversation very well—except that a fox is somehow involved—and feel a sense of shock. You still haven't taken any notes because you don't have a clue what to write. The student sitting next to you kindly shows you a textbook, open to a page that says "*Pierson v. Post*." Apparently, you were supposed to have read an assignment before class—before the very *first* class! How did those other students know that?

You begin to read, desperate to catch up. But things only get worse. The material is even more mystifying than the conversation between the professor and the student. The text is written in English but is otherwise impossible to follow. It is filled with words that are either unfamiliar or don't seem to make any sense in the context in which the words are being used. While you read, you are missing what's being said in class. Professor O'Connor has continued to ask questions of students. Sometimes they sound confident about their answers, but just as often they seem as confused as you feel. You can't figure out whether you should write down everything that is said or prepare for the possibility that she'll call on you again.

It is your first day of law school, and you are already behind.

After your first class, you find where the assignments are posted online and begin to read for your next class. But this reading is equally baffling. You can't possibly memorize everything you're reading, so how can you tell what's important? How do you determine what the "facts" and "holding" are if you're asked again (and you wonder whether a different professor *will* ask that same question)? What should you do if you don't understand a word and you can't find it in the dictionary? What is a "standard of review" or a "precedent," and how are they relevant?

This book helps you avoid this frightening prospect. It takes some of the guesswork out of the first year of law school, providing information on a variety of levels:

- Basic, like *how do I know what to read?*
- Foundational, like *why are professors asking questions instead of answering them?*
- Practical, like *what am I supposed to get out of the reading assignment?*
- Technical, like *what do those unfamiliar words and concepts mean?*

This book offers a carefully organized account of what you need to know and why. The text and graphics offer you resources to which you can turn as you prepare for classes in your first year and beyond. Frequent illustrations and exercises allow you to apply what you are learning and practice using it while you read. The book reflects input from law professors and students about what they wish first-year law students knew when they began law school.

Whether you are about to start law school or are just thinking about applying (or are curious about American legal education), this book will help. You may think that you're ready for law school. You've probably excelled at school for much of your life. You read well, have developed good study habits, and know how to learn. That's a great start, so why would you need a book to help you prepare for law school? The answer is that law school in the United States is different from any of your previous educational experiences, and not just because it is about an unfamiliar subject. The reading assignments, the classroom dynamic, the purpose of your classes, and the professors' expectations will be different from anything you have experienced before.

We have been teaching first-year law students for a combined total of more than 60 years. We understand that the first year can be intimidating, but we believe that it can also be exhilarating and rewarding. We wrote this book to reduce the intimidation and increase the excitement and satisfaction. This book helps beginning law students become productive and effective as quickly as possible. We've also included resources to help students *maintain* an edge throughout their law school careers. Think of this book as your secret guide for doing well in law school.

Chapter 1

WHAT TO EXPECT IN LAW SCHOOL

Imagine that you are suddenly sitting in the cockpit of an airplane without knowing how to fly. Some things look familiar: there is a computer screen in front of you, along with a metal object that looks like a steering wheel and dials that look vaguely like the speedometer of a car. Some things are marked with words you can read but whose meaning or use baffles you: rudder, altimeter, wind speed, ground speed. You do not know the first thing about getting the plane off the ground, much less successfully flying it—but there's no one there to help you learn.

The first year of law school in the United States, known as "1L," can feel similar. You do not know the concepts, the vocabulary, or the context for the material that you are supposed to be learning. Even if you can understand the words of a sentence, you cannot figure out what the sentence means or what you should be learning from it. This book solves that problem. We will tell you what to expect from your first year of law school, provide you with the background you need, and give you the tools to succeed.

In law school, you will learn in two primary ways: by reading and by doing. Classes are designed to teach you how to approach the law as a subject and as a practice. Professors are teaching you to "think like a lawyer." To do that, your professors will expect you to be able to *use* what you have read. In other words, you must be an active learner. You cannot expect to sit back and passively absorb information.

Law is fundamentally about solving problems. In practice, you will be solving real clients' problems. In law school, you will be solving hypothetical problems, often based on real ones. You will draw on what you have learned from assignments and class and apply that knowledge to solve a problem. Consider these examples:

- A court holds that a certain punishment attaches for people who purposely harm an animal. Does the same punishment attach to someone who lets her dog ride in the back of a pickup truck and then has a car accident in which the dog is injured? Should it matter whether the accident is her fault or not?
- A statute imposes a higher tariff on imported "dolls" than on imported "action figures." Which tariff applies to a 12-inch Harry Potter toy with a soft body and movable plastic arms, legs, and head?
- The Federal Reserve System, the central bank of the United States, issues a regulation providing that banks must make funds from an "electronic payment" available for withdrawal by "the business day after the banking day on which the bank received the electronic payment." If customers transfer money from their Venmo account to their bank account on a Friday, when can they withdraw the money? What if the bank is open on Saturday? What if a customer electronically transfers the funds from another account at the same bank?
- A cupcake shop wants to enter a contract to purchase its eggs from a farm. The cupcake shop needs fresh eggs every day but only knows how many it will need the day before it places its order. How do you draft a contract for an unspecified number of eggs, especially if you know that courts usually enforce only contracts in which a party promises to take a specific action?

These sorts of exercises require active thinking rather than passive learning, and you cannot do that just by listening and reading. Law school is about developing the abilities, tools, and processes for solving problems, and you must be an active participant in your legal education.

Law school's different focus—on learning how to be a lawyer rather than just on learning the law—is reflected in three distinct aspects of the first-year experience: the first-year curriculum, the method of classroom instruction, and material you read are all designed to serve the purposes of a legal education. All three require your active participation. The next section describes each of these aspects of your first year of law school.

THE FIRST YEAR OF LAW SCHOOL ("1L"): AN OVERVIEW

Courses Taught in the First Year (1L)

First-year courses share fundamental goals, even as they examine different areas of law. The 1L curriculum will vary slightly by law school, but the most common 1L courses are:

- Civil Procedure (often shortened to "Civ Pro") will help you understand how a lawsuit works: how parties initiate and respond to a suit (pleading), where the suit may be brought (jurisdiction), who may sue whom (joinder), how the parties obtain information (discovery), and when a case will be resolved (motions to dismiss and summary judgment). Think of it as the course for when someone says "so sue me."
- Constitutional Law (or "Con Law"), if it is taught in the first year, looks at how the U.S. Constitution allocates decision-making authority among government institutions and grants (or limits) the substantive powers of government. The 1L class may also introduce individual rights and liberties. This is the course about *who* gets to decide *what*.
- Contracts is about promises—why, when, and how to enforce them. Along with Property and Torts, Contracts is a mainstay of the 1L year and has been immortalized in books and movies as the most painful class. Typical topics include contract formation, interpretation, performance (or breach), and remedies. If someone says "but you *promised*," this course will help you respond.
- Criminal Law (or "Crim") examines criminal liability but not criminal procedure. You will likely explore the purposes of punishment and the sources and limitations of the government's

power to punish. In addition, the course will examine the relevance of mental state (or *mens rea*) and the elements (the things that have to be proven for a conviction) of specific crimes. It's the "do the crime, serve the time" course.

- **Property** considers land ownership, possession, and use. The professor may also introduce intellectual property and personal property. Common law estates as well as present and future interests in land are classic subjects in this course. Contemporary topics include landlord-tenant law, environmental law, and government regulation of land use. This is the course for the "it's mine and I can do what I want" crowd.
- **Torts** is about civil (as opposed to criminal) wrongdoing. Tort claims may arise from injuries to people or property. Your Torts class will cover strict liability and negligence (including duty, breach, and causation). The professor might also explore malpractice, products liability, defamation, and other civil wrongs for which the law gives a remedy. Torts teaches you when and how the exclamation "you hurt me!" translates into "and now you have to pay."
- **Legal Research and Writing** is typically the only 1L course that focuses directly on practical skills rather than substantive law. You will probably learn how to conduct legal research, how to write legal documents including memoranda and appellate briefs, and how to present oral arguments. The course usually covers two semesters and goes by many names.

While the first-year curriculum of law schools has remained remarkably stable over the last century, schools continuously innovate and try out new classes in the first year. Some schools have brought upper-level subjects such as international law and administrative law into the first year or created overview courses designed to provide students with a bigger picture of law and legal methods (these overview courses might be called Legal Methods, Legal Process, Legislation and Regulation, or the Regulatory State, among other names). Others offer expanded hands-on experience or some choice of elective courses in the first year. Some of these changes will stick—Civil Procedure only became a regular part of the first-year curriculum in the 1970s and now is standard—while others will evolve into something new or disappear.

Case Method

Almost all 1L classes rely on the "case method" of instruction. Instead of reading *about* the law, you will read the law itself. Your law school textbooks offer an immediate, obvious, and visible contrast between law school and undergraduate education. The books primarily contain judicial opinions, called cases,[1] which have been selected and edited by the author(s) of the textbook. The books themselves, fittingly, are called casebooks. Because judicial opinions are not the only source of law, most casebooks also contain or refer to statutes, regulations, and rules. Some may include other primary source materials, such as treaties or contracts. Casebook authors might also add commentary, questions, and information about related issues in text preceding or following the cases. But the most important material is the law itself—the cases and other primary sources—not the additional text. You will learn the law and how to think like a lawyer by studying these primary legal materials.

Law school courses use primary legal materials because lawyers do so. Remember, law school isn't just about teaching you the law, it's about teaching you how to learn and use the law. Reading cases and other primary sources helps you develop the skills you will need as a lawyer. When clients need answers to legal questions or solutions to legal problems, lawyers have to turn to the law itself: to cases, statutes, and other legal materials. Only rarely will they be able to rely on their existing knowledge or on descriptive texts.

Primary source materials, in law as in other fields, are often harder to understand than descriptive text. The purpose of descriptive text is to educate the reader. The purpose of a judicial opinion (or a statute or contract) is to accomplish a different goal. So while a legal text might describe legal doctrine, a judicial opinion decides a dispute, a statute sets the governing rules, and a contract records the agreement of the contracting parties. The opinion, statute, and contract *embody* and/or *use* legal doctrines rather than describing them.

---

1. The term "case" is used in several senses in legal education and law. In the text above, it refers to the judicial decision resolving a dispute. It can also mean the legally salient facts that resulted in the parties' dispute. The word "case" is also used to refer to the lawsuit itself (and not just the court's resolution of it), an argument supporting a particular position ("make the case for tenant"), and a criminal investigation.

Reading cases (and other legal primary sources) is a special skill. It requires you not only to understand the information conveyed, but also to extract legal principles from that information and to evaluate the source itself. We discuss each of these tasks in more detail in the next chapter, but let's begin here with the one that is probably the most unfamiliar: extracting legal principles.

Consider the following three sample legal materials that you might read for a first-year class: excerpts from a judicial opinion, a statute, and a contract. Each reflects the same legal principle. Try to identify that legal principle and state it in a simple sentence or two.

LARRY LANDLORD V. TERRY TENANT

Supreme Court of Floribama (2016)

. . . When one party breaches a contract, the other party may recover reasonable damages arising from that breach. The wronged party, however, is not ordinarily entitled to sit back and make the breaching party compensate him for losses that he can easily prevent. Thus, in circumstances such as the present case, where a tenant breaches a lease agreement, but the landlord can easily mitigate his damages by finding another tenant, he is required to do so. . . . Judgment for the defendant, Terry Tenant.

RESIDENTIAL LEASE BREACH AND MITIGATION ACT

Floribama Civil Code §1423 (2018)

Section 1. Breach; remedies. If a lease on residential property is for a period of greater than one month and the tenant repudiates the lease by (1) notifying the landlord of his intent to repudiate or (2) vacating the leased property and failing to pay one installment of the contractual lease amount, then the landlord is entitled to collect from the tenant any unpaid rent due under the lease, except as provided by Section 2.

Section 2. Mitigation. A landlord may collect unpaid rent under Section 1 only if he first takes reasonable steps to rent the property to another tenant. If he rents the property to another tenant, the amount he is entitled to collect from the breaching tenant shall be reduced by the amount of rent that he receives from the new tenant over the period of the original tenant's lease, less any sums he is required to expend to make the property habitable after the departure of the original tenant.

HOLMES PLACE APARTMENTS LEASE AGREEMENT

Paragraph 27. If the tenant fails to pay rent, the landlord is entitled to evict the tenant, to re-rent the property to another, and to collect from the tenant any unpaid rent not obtained through subsequent rental. The landlord must make a reasonable effort to lease the property to a substitute tenant.

It would have been a lot easier if we had simply described the principle: tenants who break their leases are liable to the landlord for the remaining unpaid rent, but the landlord is required to try to find another tenant to relieve the first tenant from all or part of the obligation. (Did you identify that principle? Don't worry if you didn't—this book and your first-year classes will help you develop that skill.)

If we had given you a textual description instead of the primary sources, you would have learned *only* the principle, that is, only the basic legal doctrine. That knowledge might have helped you advise a client who wanted to break a lease or a landlord whose tenant had done so, but it would have been utterly useless for any other purpose. Wrestling with the language of the law—the opinion, the statute, and the contract—was much more valuable because it began the process of teaching you how to read and learn from legal materials on other topics. For these reasons, the case method—reading cases and other legal sources—has become one of the hallmarks of American legal education.

Socratic Method

The Socratic method is the second hallmark of American law schools. This teaching strategy relies on a dialogue between the teacher and the student, earning it the name of the Greek philosopher who invented the pedagogical style. The professor asks sustained and increasingly penetrating questions of students rather than lecturing on the cases that the students have read.

In the paradigmatic form, the professor begins by calling on a student without warning. The student is first asked to "state" (or "recite") "the case"—to describe as succinctly and precisely as possible the key facts of the dispute, the issue addressed by the court's decision, and the resolution of this issue. The professor then asks a series of follow-up questions, each building on the student's answer to the prior question. "Why?" is the most common question. The professor will eventually focus on the basis for the court's decision, and slowly and carefully try to unpack the court's reasoning by revealing its assumptions and implications. The court is unlikely to have answered most of these questions—at least not explicitly. To answer them, then, you will have to read the court's opinion actively and critically.

While this is an accurate description of the Socratic method in general, individual professors vary in every aspect of the method. For example, professors may not rely on true "cold calling"—calling on random students without warning. Some will assign students to panels that will be "on-call" on specified days. Others will rely (mostly) on volunteers. They may call on students alphabetically or according to where they are seated. Despite these variations, most professors still rely on the element of surprise at least some of the time, so you should always be prepared to be in the "hot seat."

The pattern of questioning also might vary. Here are some examples of the questions a professor might ask in a class discussing the *Landlord v. Tenant* case we excerpted earlier:

- What is the **issue**? (A: Must the tenant pay the rent?)
- What is the **holding**? (A: The tenant need not pay the rent because the landlord did not try to find a replacement tenant.)

- What is the **legal rule** or **principle**? (A: A landlord must try to mitigate damages by finding a replacement tenant.)
- Does the legal rule **apply** to other types of parties or contracts? For example, what should happen if a parts supplier breaches a sales contract with a manufacturer by failing to supply parts needed in the production of the manufacturer's goods? (A: Maybe the manufacturer should have to try to find the parts elsewhere before suing for breach. It depends on how broadly the principle reaches—which is likely to be the next question, regardless of how you answer this one!)
- How is the judicial case different from the statute? (A: One important difference is that the statute applies only to landlords and thus does not apply to other types of parties like the manufacturer in our example above. By contrast, the legal principle expressed in the court's opinion may be relevant in other contract disputes, including the hypothetical dispute between the parts supplier and the manufacturer.)
- **Why** should a landlord (or other non-breaching party) have to take steps to mitigate—does such a rule let the breaching party off too easy? (A: It depends on what the law governing breach of contract should be trying to accomplish—again, a natural follow-up question.)

Some professors might start with the first of these questions, or with even more basic questions; others might jump directly to the later questions.

All of these sorts of questions require you to *think*—to actively engage with ideas—at two different points in time. First, you should come to class having thought about the reading and having tried to anticipate the professor's questions (we'll help you learn to do that in later chapters). But you will also have to think *in* class before answering a question. You should not assume that the answer to a question is somewhere in the casebook or in your notes. A Socratic class is not about regurgitating what you have read or learned; it is about helping you to "think like a lawyer." The professor's job is to direct and channel your thinking.

Socratic dialogue and the case method define American legal education. And because they are rarely used outside of law schools, you may wonder why we use them. We do so because they are effective at accomplishing the goals of law school that we mentioned at the outset of this chapter. As one anonymous reviewer of Langdell's Contracts casebook noted, the purpose of this type of legal instruction "is to teach the student the habit of legal analysis and synthesis, not to make the student's mind a mere dictionary of decisions." (Book Review, *Langdell's "Selected Cases on Contracts,"* 6 Southern L. Rev. n.s. 448, 449 (1880).) Using both Socratic questioning and primary legal sources instills the type of close analysis required for legal work.

The Socratic method is probably unfamiliar to you, and you may find it difficult at first. You may become frustrated by the professor's failure to give an answer to the big questions that the professor asks. You will find it less frustrating if you remember that the professor isn't hiding the ball when refusing to provide an answer—in fact, the lack of an answer *is* the answer. Legal rules and legal analysis rarely produce unequivocal answers, and you should not expect to learn law the way you might memorize chemical formulas or historical facts. While a court may declare a rule in a particular opinion, the debate over whether that was the correct conclusion will continue. Moreover, questions will remain as to whether the rule should apply in a slightly different or new setting. Finally, law school exams—to say nothing of legal practice—require you to recognize and deal with ambiguity and uncertainty: to figure out whether there is an easy answer and what to do if there is no easy answer. In many ways, puzzling out the ambiguities in the law is the fun and creative part of learning the law!

Some of you will enjoy being called on and speaking in class. For others, speaking in front of so many classmates may be embarrassing, even painful. To those who dread being called on, we encourage you to relax. The purpose of this means of instruction is for you to learn and improve. You *will* make mistakes. There is nothing wrong with making mistakes, only with failing to learn from them. Try to view speaking in class as an opportunity to improve your mental acuity and analytic skill. Your professors want you to learn, and they will try to tailor their questions to help you do so, even (or especially) if you start out with a wrong answer. We promise that you are far more likely than your classmates or teachers to remember your mistakes or verbal stumbles. And because effective communication—to clients, judges, and other lawyers—is an important key to succeeding as a lawyer, speaking in class will help you improve your legal skills.

The Socratic method can be difficult for students and professors alike. Students who are being closely questioned are often uncomfortable, even if they are learning. Their classmates may feel their pain, or classmates may be bored or frustrated if they think they know the answers (be careful—we put "think" in this sentence for a reason!). The professor cannot rely on a prepared lecture but must be ready for any response and tailor the next question to the last response. A Socratic class also covers much less material than a lecture class. Some professors (including the two authors of this book) believe that the pedagogical advantages of the Socratic method outweigh these disadvantages, but others reach a different conclusion. Some of your professors may lecture instead of or in addition to using Socratic questioning.

Whatever form your classes take, be an active participant. Listen critically to the professor and your classmates. Do you agree with what is said? Can you answer the questions that are asked—even if you are not in the hot seat? Do not take verbatim notes. Trying to type everything that's said (or even everything the professor says) will prevent you from *thinking* while in class, and you will miss a crucial part of the classroom experience.

SUCCEEDING IN LAW SCHOOL FROM THE FIRST DAY

Preparing for Class

Preparing for law school classes is not like preparing for undergraduate or graduate school classes. For one thing, legal writing is not like other types of writing: it is more precise, more carefully structured, and more densely packed with information. Thus, legal reading is not like other types of reading. We cannot emphasize too strongly how crucial it is to learn how to read cases and other legal sources accurately and efficiently.

Legal reading is a difficult skill to develop. Improving reading proficiency is a continuous process. While the good reading skills that you have developed prior to law school will serve as a solid foundation, they are simply that: a start. They will not be sufficient. Indeed, numerous reading strategies that are highly effective when reading textbooks in other fields are not useful in law and can even be counterproductive.

Every word matters, and skimming, relying on paragraph structure (such as topic sentences), focusing on key words or terms, and the like will not work in law school.

As you read for class, you should keep in mind the three primary objectives of law school, especially of the first year:

1. Students should *understand* legal doctrines.
2. Students should be able to *use* legal doctrines.
3. Students should be able to *extend their knowledge* of legal doctrines on their own.

While all three objectives are important, they are not equally important during the 1L year. Developing the ability to *use* the law is the most important, and *understanding* legal doctrines themselves is the least important (learning legal doctrines increases in importance in the second and third years, especially as you become better at using the law and at learning the law on your own).

In the next chapter, we will talk more specifically about how to read in order to accomplish these three tasks. But keeping these goals in mind, as well as always remembering that you will be using the law to solve problems, will help you focus on the big picture as you read and "brief" cases (briefing is also discussed in the next chapter). You want to read actively and with a purpose—and part of your job is to figure out what that purpose is for each reading assignment.

In the meantime, here are a few quick and easy things you can do from day one to prepare for class successfully.

- Break your bad reading habits cold turkey. Do you surf the web, check e-mail, or watch TV while you read assignments? Stop!
- Don't skim. Whatever you've done before, you can't get by in law school by picking out a few apparently[2] significant phrases and skimming the rest.
- Use a dictionary. There will be many unfamiliar terms in your reading assignments. Don't just gloss over them. Look them up in either a regular dictionary or a legal dictionary. You can find many dictionaries online. Even just using Google will probably produce results.

2. We use "apparently" advisedly: just because the phrase *looks* insignificant doesn't mean it is. And always read the footnotes in your casebook—they're there for a reason. (Get it?)

- Get used to uncertainty and ambiguity. More often than not, a case or a statute can be interpreted in multiple ways. There are few clear answers to legal questions. That is what makes the study of law an incredible and exciting challenge.

In Class

In the next chapter, we will talk more about how to get the most out of each class, but we start here with some fundamentals. First and foremost, you should *always* attend class, even if you did not always do so as an undergraduate. Studies of law student performance find that successful students attend class more regularly than their less successful peers. The relationship between class attendance and student performance is complex. When you attend class, you learn more than you would by studying cases alone. Judicial opinions are difficult to dissect and digest. Classroom discussion will improve your understanding of a specific case and make you a better legal thinker. The Socratic method and class discussion will help you learn to *use* the law instead of just reading about it. You also receive information in an alternate form when you attend class—you hear the information spoken and consider it in a dynamic environment. Thus, class attendance can improve your performance through the information it provides, the method of dissemination, and the structure of class time.

As a matter of courtesy to the professor and to other students, you should always be on time. If you need to boot up a laptop or remove material from your backpack, you should arrive early enough to do so *before* the class is scheduled to start. At the scheduled time, you should be in your seat ready to begin, with your books and notes in front of you, open to the appropriate page. And you should always bring tangible writing material (a pen or pencil and paper) even if you take notes on a laptop or tablet, in case your device fails or there is a diagram or other material that might be difficult to transcribe.

You should be an active listener in class in the same way that you were an active reader when preparing for class. Let's start with the simple things. Sit attentively and focus on the speakers. Listen with curiosity to both the professor and your classmates. Tune out everything else, and turn off cell phones, the Internet, and e-mail. Studies have shown that even for adept multitaskers like most of you, performance on difficult mental tasks is slowed by distractions. Some distractions, such as a ringing phone or a computer game on a laptop screen, are also disruptive to others.

Now that you are focused on class, you need to adapt your note-taking habits to law school. You should *not* simply transcribe the professor's words and the dialogue with your classmates. One of the dangers of laptop computers is that, depending on your typing speed, you can record verbatim what is said in class. But you shouldn't! You should mostly be listening. As you listen, you should be thinking, prioritizing, and putting into your notes the most important themes and ideas, the ones that are key to understanding the material. You should be paraphrasing—writing in your own words your understanding of what they are saying. When you aren't sure what something means, make a note to yourself to find out. Critical listening requires engagement with what you hear.

The point of the Socratic dialogue is to lead students to an understanding of the material and how to use it. If you write down every question and answer, some of the answers will be wrong or misleading because they will be corrected later in the dialogue. You also will end up with so many notes that they will be useless for review purposes. And if you wait for the professor to signal that the right answer has been reached, that may never happen: either there is no right answer, or the professor wants the students to recognize it on their own. Besides, law school isn't about *right* answers, it's about the *process* of getting to them.

So, what should you be doing in class? You should be following along with the discussion or with the student who is in the hot seat: think about how you would answer the professor's questions, and when a student answers, evaluate the answer and think about what you would ask next.

You should also try to participate in class even when you are not in the hot seat, but do so judiciously. First, do not try to preempt the Socratic dialogue or rescue the student who is being questioned. A professor who would like volunteers will say so (and not all floundering students will welcome your attempt to help!). Second, think about what you want to say before you raise your hand. Third, do not monopolize the conversation: if you find that your hand is often in the air, but you are not being called on (or are always being called on last), you are talking too much. Fourth, be sure to listen to other students' comments and questions, and do not say the same thing in different words.

A few final words on hypotheticals or "hypos": a professor, especially in 1L courses, will often describe a hypothetical case and ask how it should be decided in light of the material that you have read or studied earlier in the hour or the semester. Sometimes the professor might ask you to represent a particular position and give the strongest arguments on that side. This is your best opportunity to learn how to "think like a lawyer." It is also the classroom activity that is most similar to what lawyers do: they apply existing law to new facts, sometimes to advise clients and sometimes to advocate on their behalf. As we will discuss shortly, most law school exams are also basically extended hypotheticals, so exploring hypotheticals in class is good practice for the final exam. You should be hungry for hypos—answer (at least in your head) every one, make up your own, and think about potential hypos as you read.

Outside of Class

Learning a specific topic doesn't end when the class period spent on that topic is over. After class ends, you should review and organize your notes, integrating those from the most recent class with your notes from prior classes. Reviewing your notes away from class will reveal points and connections that weren't previously apparent and help you to absorb new ideas. It is the best way to begin preparing for the next class session, and it also will make it easier to prepare for the final exam.

In reviewing your notes, you might find that you have questions. Perhaps you missed something in class or didn't completely understand it. You should first reread the relevant assigned material to see if it resolves the difficulty. If not, talk to your classmates—you will all benefit if you pool your knowledge.

You might also decide to work with classmates on a regular basis either in a formal study group or in informal discussions. Talking with other students is a great way to think through the material and to examine it from different perspectives. If you can explain an idea or issue to someone else, then you truly understand it. And you can come up with hypotheticals for each other and work through them together. Thus, working in groups can be highly beneficial. But it also can be very time-consuming. You should be vigilant about the time you spend discussing material with others. Don't forget to keep enough time to go over it again on your own. Time management is a constant challenge in law school, but especially during your first year.

If you still have questions, consider using published materials created by legal experts and aimed at law students and other similarly situated users. The most exhaustive subject-specific books are **treatises.** Also known as **hornbooks** (because they were originally bound in animal-horn covers), treatises are comprehensive and detailed examinations of a specific legal subject that generally is the focus of a same-named course. (In Contracts, for example, *Corbin on Contracts* is perhaps the best known.) Hornbooks offer a valuable resource for selective study when you wish to gain a deeper understanding of a doctrine or when you need additional illustrations of how the doctrine is applied. But they generally are too detailed to be a regular study aid during your first year of law school.

There are also books created just for law students. As a sign of the difficulty of law school (and the drive of law students), this market is remarkably large and the demand appears to be insatiable. **Commercial study aids** appear in different formats:

- commercial outlines (such as Gilbert's or Emanuel's) that offer annotated outlines of various legal subjects;
- canned briefs that provide minimal breakdowns of cases into some of their parts (not always correctly);
- primers (such as the Essentials, Nutshells, and Understandings series), which provide abridged overviews of various legal subjects and their crucial aspects; and
- question-and-answer texts that teach the information through a series of hypotheticals (or questions) and corresponding analysis (such as Examples & Explanations and Questions & Answers).

Study aids appear to give "answers," but they will short-circuit your learning process. Similar cautions apply to outlines, class notes, or other material you might obtain from upper-class students who have previously taken the course, and to online resources such as Wikipedia and blog posts. Remember, developing legal analytic skills is the primary purpose of the first year of law school. If you rely on someone else's distillation of case or concept, you will not master the skills and techniques that come from grappling with material on your own and working through difficult questions in class. They can also be distracting, containing material that the professor doesn't expect you to know or explaining it in ways that differ from the professor's methods (plus, you'd be surprised to discover how much misleading and even incorrect information is in them!).

So be very careful about your use of any external summary. Every year, we see too many 1L students who think they are well prepared because they have obtained (and memorized) substantive legal doctrine from some outside source and who end up disappointed in their grades. This is especially true when the "study aid" is an outline prepared by a student in a previous year's class. Don't be tempted to follow someone else's outline just because many of your classmates are doing so! Remember, it's the *process*, not the answers, that matters most.

If you still have questions, you can always ask your professor as a last resort. Be sure to be aware of each professor's policies on office hours, e-mail questions, and the like; that information is probably on the syllabus or posted on the class webpage. Most professors are happy to answer questions and assist you in understanding the material. But we expect you to try to resolve your questions first by yourself or with classmates before you come to us. You will learn the material only by working through it on your own—that's why asking the professor should be your last option rather than your first.

Respect your professors' time. If you do need help from your professors, be well prepared prior to asking them questions and be thoughtful about the time that you're taking. For example, if you miss class or miss something that was said in class, find out what you missed by asking a classmate, not by asking the professor to fill you in.

Law School Exams

Most professors rely heavily—if not entirely—on a *single* final exam as the basis for your course grade. Law school exams will likely be very different from any exams that you have taken before. The exam will last several hours or even a full day. It will include essay questions and/or multiple-choice questions. The prototypical law school essay question is an **issue-spotter**: the professor creates a complex hypothetical scenario and asks you to evaluate fully the legal issues raised by the facts. Professors may also ask a theory or policy question, but these are less common and, even when used, less important to your grade. The exam may be open-book (you may access outside materials), closed-book (it is just you and the exam), or hybrid. You should find out as soon as possible how the professor intends to grade your class performance as the method of testing should influence your method of preparation.

Exam preparation will be centered around outlining. **Outlining** is the process of organizing, digesting, and condensing your notes and other class materials. An outline is not just a list of cases or classes, but a synthesis of all of the concepts and material you have been learning. You will review the outline before the exam and may be able to use it in the exam itself (if the exam is open-book). But the act of creating an outline is as important as the tangible product. You will truly learn the subject through this process of identifying and developing the strands of thought running through the assigned reading, outside materials, and your class notes, and then figuring out how to weave those strands together. Be sure to use the outlining process to focus on the legal principles, not just the specific facts of each case. And as you construct your outline, think about the big picture: how the entire body of law that you have been studying in that class comes together.

Professors may provide you with a preview of the final exam by administering a practice exam or offering old exams for review. A **practice exam** is just that: a mini-version of the final exam that does not affect your grade and that is given during the term. The professor may provide individualized feedback or offer a model answer. Old exams, by contrast, are actual copies of an exam previously given by the professor in the same class. The professor may include a model answer or samples of good student answers along with the old exams. Practice exams and old exams allow you to anticipate the final exam's structure and format. And they give you an opportunity to practice, make mistakes, and improve. It is often helpful to take old (or practice) exams under realistic conditions: limit yourself to the time allotted and actually write out your answers, then compare them to the models. If there are no model answers, study groups can be particularly productive as a way to consider what constitutes good answers.

When it comes to taking the real exam, time management is the most important issue. Do not be misled by the open-book format into assuming that you will have time to consult your notes and book. Few exams allow enough time for it. You will be rushed to address the exam's numerous issues. No exam answer is perfect. Indeed, a top exam in the class may catch only 60 percent of the arguments.

The purpose of final exams should inform your approach to final exams. Just as with reading and listening, you should approach your answers to final exam questions mindful of why you are undertaking this task. The professor wants to see how well you understand the material covered in the course *and* how well you can use that material to solve problems. Remember that in addition to learning a substantive area of law, you are supposed to be learning how to analyze and reason. The professor wants to see you make arguments, calling upon your substantive knowledge in the context of the exam questions. Read the questions carefully. Your answer should be responsive to the question that the professor asked and should take into account all relevant information offered by the professor. This is another reason that class attendance is helpful: how professors teach a subject reflects how they understand it. Their exam questions, as well as their grading of the answers, will reflect that understanding. This is another reason to be wary of study aids, too. Chapter 2 will explain how to develop the reading and writing skills that are crucial to success on law school exams. For a comprehensive and innovative guide to taking law school exams, you should consult Barry Friedman & John C.P. Goldberg, *Open Book: The Inside Track to Law School Success* (2d ed., Aspen 2016).

BEGIN YOUR LEGAL EDUCATION WITH THIS BOOK

Now that you know what to expect in the first year of law school, how should you prepare for it? Reading this book—actively!—is a good start. We have designed the book both to give you the background and tools you'll need during your first year and to ease you into the kind of reading and thinking that will be expected of you. In this section, we explain how to get the most out of this book, and then give some preliminary advice for your very first day of law school.

As you read this book:

- Think critically by evaluating what you read, asking questions as you read, and considering how you might answer those questions.
- Use every opportunity we provide to test and apply your new knowledge.
- Look up any unfamiliar words—if you cannot find them in a standard dictionary, try a legal dictionary such as *Black's Law Dictionary*.
- Compare the graphics to the textual explanations. Make sure you understand how they relate to each other.
- Answer the questions posed in the text and do all the "Test Your Understanding" exercises. We've put answers to the "Test Your Understanding" exercises in the back of the book—but don't peek until you've thoroughly thought out your own answer!

Reading this book in these ways will serve as practice for reading assignments in your first-year courses. You learn by doing.

Chapter 2 focuses on the critical skills necessary to understanding and using the language of the law. We will show you how to read and annotate assigned materials, how to take notes in class, and how to communicate in class and in written assignments (including exams).

Learning the *language* of the law is not enough to give you an edge. Many professors seem to assume that students arrive at law school with *background knowledge* about the American legal system, and about tools and concepts ranging from principles of economics to basic legal terminology. They refer to or rely on such knowledge without ever actually teaching it to you! This book fills the gap, giving you a chance to gain the background knowledge that will help you succeed in law school.

We start with a guide to American government and law in Chapter 3 and then focus in greater detail on the American legal system in Chapter 4. The material covered in these two chapters may be familiar to you. If you are such a reader, use these chapters to review and focus your knowledge. For other readers, the material will be entirely new. If that's you, use the material as an introduction. Most of you will fall in between, recognizing some, but not all, of the material.

Chapter 5 discusses fundamental concepts that are important for understanding law and legal analysis. Most of it will probably be unfamiliar to you. This information will help bring you up to speed if the professor—or assigned reading material—refers to such concepts as "standards of review," "balancing tests," "burdens of proof," or "expected value."

How should you approach all this background information? There is certainly too much to memorize. Instead, approach it—*and approach all your reading during law school*—by categorizing it according to its importance and adjusting your focus accordingly. It might help to divide the material into four categories:

- Direct Knowledge. Things you need to know cold. You should be able to recall and use this information automatically without looking it up. As you learn "black-letter law" (that is, the statements of legal principles that you will use to answer legal questions), you will have to incorporate that into your direct knowledge. Statements like "a contract requires consideration," or "a court has personal jurisdiction over the defendant if the defendant has minimum contacts with the forum state" are examples of black-letter law. Black-letter law doesn't answer very many questions (What counts as consideration? How many contacts, and what kind, are enough?) but you need to start with it and know it cold.
- General Knowledge. Things you need to be generally familiar with but need not know in detail. As the details become important later in your legal education or career, this general knowledge will give you the basis for understanding and absorbing them.
- Available Knowledge. Things that you do not need to carry in your head but do need to be able to find when needed.
- Examples. Things that are not directly relevant but are included to illustrate or add color to the text.

Focus more on the first two categories, marking the relevant portions of the text so you can review them later. (Then review them later!) Make a mental note of items in the third category. Use the last category to help you understand the material or to make it easier to remember.

Test Your Understanding

Reread the first section of this chapter ("The First Year of Law School ("IL"): An Overview"). Break the material down into the categories of direct knowledge, general knowledge, available knowledge, and examples.

In Chapter 6, we provide a "cheat sheet" on theoretical and historical concepts lurking in your law school classes. We offer an abbreviated review of American history and basic legal theories, homing in on the ideas and information that will be useful to you as you prepare for and participate in class.

AFTER YOU FINISH THIS BOOK

Many of you will read this book before you begin your first day of law school. We hope that it can also serve as a resource throughout law school. But what else should you do to prepare yourself for your first day of classes? Some things are obvious: make sure you know where you are supposed to go and allow enough time to get there. We have had students oversleep, get lost on their way to the law school, fail to find a parking place, or go to the wrong room. You do not want to be the student who walks in late on the first day of class—that is not the reputation you want to begin earning.

You should also know that law school courses usually do not start as gently as college courses. There is no "introductory" day in law school—you cover substantive material from the very first class. You should not assume, as Mr. Hart did in *The Paper Chase,* that the first class "would be a lecture—an introduction to the course." As the legendary Professor Kingsfield admonished the humiliated Hart, "Never assume anything in my classroom!" (*The Paper Chase* (20th Century Fox 1973)). You will want to prepare—and prepare fully—for your first class (and the later ones, too).

Shortly before classes begin, professors will post your first reading assignments on the course website. If the professor has taken the time to post information, then they will assume that you know it. While your professor probably won't ask *you,* as Professor Stromwell asked Elle Woods, "to leave class and to return only when [you are] prepared," why take the chance? (*Legally Blonde* (MGM 2001)).

In class, you want to be prepared to answer questions whether directed at you or a classmate. You should listen closely to the exchange between the professor and a student. You are all learning from and with each other. Do not make the mistake of interrupting a dialogue with another student. As Professor Keating warned, "Never take a learning opportunity away from another student. No matter how smart you need everyone to think you are." (*How to Get Away with Murder* (ABC Studios, Season 1, Episode 1, 2014)).

Law school—learning the law and how to think like a lawyer—is an exciting, fun, and rich experience. But as we explained, it is also a challenging, demanding, and difficult one. We firmly believe that preparation—including reading this book—will help you to be a more productive, more effective, and ultimately happier law student and lawyer. Let's get started!

Chapter 2

THE LANGUAGE OF THE LAW

Lawyers are problem solvers. Lawyers solve problems through careful attention to language: interpreting words and choosing words. Lawyering, then, is about language. Law school focuses on honing the skills necessary to understand and use language effectively.

In law school, you will be reading the same sorts of documents that lawyers use to solve problems, including cases, statutes, rules, and regulations. You also will review work produced by lawyers: contracts, correspondence, pleadings, and wills. These are primary source material—not a textbook or article reviewing the original material but the actual material itself. Reading legal primary source materials is not like reading novels or even textbooks (including this one!). You cannot skim to get the gist of a legal document: every **word matters.**

Law school, especially in the first year, teaches you to read, understand, and use legal texts. As a law student, you should be thinking about language at four different times: (1) when you first read legal materials, (2) when you prepare for class, (3) when you are in class, and (4) when you communicate about the law.

1. Read: As you read the assigned material, you must be actively focused on the language of the document you are reading. You will be identifying the important phrases and extracting relevant principles.

2. Prepare: As you prepare for class, you must translate the language of the document into your own words. Paraphrasing and interpreting lead to understanding and allow critical evaluation.

3. Engage: As you engage with the law in class, you will be taking notes that thoughtfully expand on what you've already learned. Class is not about information transmission. Professors are instead helping you use the information you have already learned in preparing for class.

4. Communicate: When you communicate, the language that *you* use matters. Whether you are responding to questions in class, composing a research memo, or writing an exam answer, clarity and precision are paramount.

This chapter lays out how to develop these four skills. *Reading* like a lawyer includes three steps of reading and two methods of reasoning. *Preparing* for class means annotating the material and preparing "briefs." *Engaging* in class requires thoughtful notetaking rather than mere transcribing. And *communicating* (in and out of class) demands organization, precision, and conciseness.

READING LIKE A LAWYER

First-year law students routinely overestimate their understanding of a reading assignment. How can you avoid this common problem? You must monitor your comprehension *as you read*. Be an *active* reader! Active reading means reading with a strategy and purpose.

And it means regularly reviewing what you've read and taking stock of what you've learned.

- Read, reread, and reread again. You must read every case, statute, rule, and regulation multiple times. Your approach may change with each read, but you still need to reread frequently. Law school reading assignments are shorter than undergraduate assignments because law professors multiply the assigned number of pages by the number of times you will have to reread them to understand. Keep in mind that even experienced lawyers—including your professors—regularly reread legal documents in order to comprehend them.
- Allow plenty of time. Given the density of the material and the need to read the assignment multiple times, you should expect to spend at least three or four hours preparing for every hour of class.
- Take notes. Each time you read and reread, you should be making notes for yourself. Note-taking helps you learn and remember what you are reading.

Reading like a lawyer is a **three-step process:**

1. **examine** the context,
2. **extract** the legal principles,
3. **evaluate** the reasoning.

If you learn to follow the steps in order, you will become a successful reader.

Step One: Examine the Context

The first step is to examine the context: the context of the assignment and the context of the legal material itself. We focus here on cases because they are the most common type of legal material assigned in law school, but the principles apply to any primary source legal material.

Why are you reading this case? Why has the professor assigned this particular case at this particular point in the course? What are you supposed to learn from it? You will revise your answer to this question after you read the case for the first time. But you should already have an initial answer before you begin reading the assignment.

Start with the subject of the course itself. If it's Civil Procedure and the case is about a judge dismissing a lawsuit filed by a fired worker claiming her employer discriminated against her, you are less likely to be looking for the law on discrimination and more likely to be looking for what procedures were or weren't followed and why that matters. On the other hand, in a Contracts class, the fact that a case was decided by a judge rather than a jury may matter less than exactly what that judge decided. (Don't ignore these other aspects of the case; just keep in mind that they are probably going to be less important.) Many cases involve more than one legal topic, but not all of them are equally important for each class.

Test Your Understanding

You are reading a case called *Carnival Cruise Line v. Shute*, in which a passenger sued a cruise line for injuries that occurred on board one of the line's ships. You find that early in the opinion, the court quotes the following language from the cruise ticket:

> It is agreed by and between the passenger and the Cruise Line that all disputes and matters whatsoever arising under, in connection with or incident to the Contract shall be litigated, if at all, in and before a Court located in the State of Florida, U.S.A., to the exclusion of Courts of any other state or country.

Imagine, first, that you are reading this case for your Contracts class. Then imagine that you are reading it for your Civil Procedure class instead. For each class, identify the likely purposes for reading the case—that is, the questions you might expect the case to answer.

To understand the context even more fully, you can start by looking at the casebook's table of contents. The *Carnival Cruise Line* case from the *Test Your Understanding* problem appears in your Contracts casebook in a chapter on "Contract Interpretation." In your Civil Procedure casebook, it is in the chapter on "Jurisdiction." Subheadings might narrow your focus even further: for Contracts, it's in "Form Contracts," and for Civil Procedure, it's in "Consent and Waiver." Now you know you should be reading the case in Contracts to see how it interprets form contracts. In Civil Procedure, you should be reading it to learn what it says about consenting to jurisdiction.

Also consult your syllabus and recent assignments. What topics have you been studying in the class? Is this case a continuation of an old topic or the beginning of a new topic? What else has been assigned for the same day or the same week? Does one assigned case cite another assigned case, or an assigned statute?

What is the particular context of this case? You can learn a lot from headings and notations at the beginning of a case. Consider this excerpt from the beginning of a case as it would appear in a casebook:

> *YATES V. UNITED STATES*
>
> Supreme Court of the United States
> 135 S. Ct. 1074 (2015)
>
> Justice Ginsburg announced the judgment of the Court and delivered an opinion, in which The Chief Justice, Justice Breyer, and Justice Sotomayor join.
>
> John Yates, a commercial fisherman, caught undersized red grouper in federal waters in the Gulf of Mexico. To prevent federal authorities from confirming that he had harvested undersized fish, Yates ordered a crew member to toss the suspect catch into the sea. For this offense, he was charged with, and convicted of, violating 18 U.S.C. §1519.

Many law students are tempted to skip straight to the story of John Yates and his undersized grouper. Don't fall into that trap! Everything preceding Yates's story is also important. Here's what you need to learn about a case's context from this preliminary information:

- **The court.** Which court issued this opinion? Is it a state court or a federal court? Is it a trial court or appellate court? Is it the highest court in the jurisdiction or a lower court? (Chapter 4 explains how to answer those questions.) *Yates* was decided by the Supreme Court of the United States, which is a federal appellate court and the top court on questions of federal law.

- The date. *Yates* was decided in 2015. If you are reading other cases on the same topic, you can now place *Yates* in the chronological development of a particular body of law. The date can also give you other relevant information about the world in which the dispute arose and was resolved. If the date is before 1900, you may find the case harder to read because of the style of writing. Cases decided during particular historical eras might be influenced by jurisprudential currents of the era, and you might therefore find similarities among contemporaneous cases even on different topics.
- The parties. The identity of the parties will affect how you read and interpret the case. This is a dispute between an individual, John Yates, and the government of the United States. Lawsuits between the state and a private citizen can be governed by different rules than suits between two private citizens, or disputes involving a corporation or other organization.
- The judge(s) and the number and kind of opinion. Who decided this dispute? Was the case heard by one judge or by a multi-judge panel? Was it unanimous? Which judge wrote the opinion? Which judge(s) joined it? *Yates* is particularly complicated because you see that Justice Ginsburg "announced the judgment" for the whole Supreme Court, but her opinion is only for three named Justices besides herself. Since the Supreme Court has nine justices, her opinion isn't even for a majority! That should alert you that there will be other opinions to watch out for. Those opinions might be *concurring*, *concurring in the judgment only*, or *dissenting* (or some combination, such as *dissenting in part*). (Chapter 4 explains the composition of the U.S. Supreme Court and the types of opinions issued by judges.)
- The topic. Once you get the preliminary information, your first (relatively quick) reading of the body of the case should tell you what the case is about both factually and legally. This case appears to be about whether someone who dumps undersized fish overboard can be charged under a particular federal statute, 18 U.S.C. §1519 (Chapter 4 explains that "U.S.C." is the United States Code, which contains federal statutes). So now

you know you need to find out what the Court says about the meaning of that statute and whether it applies to fish-dumping.

- The outcome. Your first reading should also yield information about what happened in this case. What did the court decide? Who won? Surprisingly, students regularly forget to figure out the outcome. It is usually at the very *end* of the case, although the Court may give you a hint early on. After the excerpt you have, the *Yates* opinion quotes the statute—which punishes the destruction of "tangible objects"—and then notes that "A tangible object captured by §1519, we hold, must be one used to record or preserve information."

Test Your Understanding

Based on the additional quotation we just provided, who won the case?

You will need to read the entire case once through to complete your contextual background on the outcome. The outcome is often announced in the very last paragraph of the opinion. Justice Ginsburg's opinion in *Yates* ends: "The judgment of the U.S. Court of Appeals for the Eleventh Circuit is therefore reversed, and the case is remanded for further proceedings." So now you know that the Supreme Court *reversed* another court (found it was incorrect), and *remanded* (sent it back to that court). With that additional information, the two sentences together tell you who won, and what the Court actually did.

Step Two: Extract the Legal Principles

Now you are ready to read the case a second time in order to derive the central legal principles. Keep two facts in mind as you read this time:

- The cases in a casebook are (almost always) *edited*. What remains should be important. It is either independently significant or necessary to understand statements which are significant.

- Keep an eye out for *footnotes* and *separate opinions*. These are usually deleted. So, if they are included, they should be read closely. Concurring or dissenting opinions may help you to understand the majority opinion and/or signal how the current case relates to past or future cases. It may also provide alternative ways of conceptualizing the issue, the doctrine, or the principles at hand.

Extracting requires that you "**brief**" the case. To brief a case means to identify, in your own words, the following four pieces of information:

- The relevant facts of the case: what happened in the world to cause the dispute?
- The procedural posture of the case: who sued whom on what claim? How did the claim reach the court whose opinion you are reading—was it filed there, or did it come from another court or an administrative agency? If the opinion is from an appellate court, what did the lower court decide and why? What is the outcome—that is, who won and what did the court order to be done?
- The court's holding: what is the court's pivotal legal conclusion? The answer may not be obvious.
- The court's reasoning: why did the court reach the result it did? This is usually the most important aspect of the case, so make sure that you understand it fully.

In order to identify these four aspects of a case, you must understand two crucial distinctions: the difference between **law** and **fact** and the difference between **substance** and **procedure**.

Facts are the real events that have occurred in the world. **Law** is how society chooses to respond to those facts—how society governs and adjusts the relationships among people given the factual events. In trial, the essential difference is between what happens *outside* the courtroom (facts) and what happens *inside* the courtroom (law).[1]

Law can be further separated into **substance** and **procedure**. Substance (or **substantive law**) creates and controls rights and obligations. Procedure (or **procedural law**) defines and describes the process by which parties protect their rights or enforce others' obligations. The substantive law of the decision is what the parties care

1. The distinction between law and fact is slippery. Some questions are even recognized as "mixed questions of law and fact."

about: what do they want? What did the court give them? The procedure is how the parties get what they want: who sued? Where? What did that initial decision-maker decide? How did the case get to the point at which you're reading it?

Now you can focus on the real purpose of your second reading: to extract the legal principles from the case. *Why* does the court reach the outcome it does? You will be looking for relevant language, rules, tests—anything that explains the reasoning that led the court to its ultimate conclusion. Sometimes the court will help you by including a sentence that starts "The rule is . . ." or "The test is . . ." Be sure to mark that sentence so you can find it! But sometimes, the test or reasoning will simply be stated, "A tangible object . . . must be one used to record or preserve information," and you will have to *identify* it as the test or reasoning.

Let's look at *Yates v. United States* as it would appear in a casebook. We have marked what you should learn from your second reading.

YATES V. UNITED STATES
Supreme Court of the United States
135 S. Ct. 1074 (2015)

CAPTION

Justice Ginsburg announced the judgment of the Court and delivered an opinion, in which The Chief Justice, Justice Breyer, and Justice Sotomayor join.

PLURALITY OPINION[2]

John Yates, a commercial fisherman, caught undersized red grouper in federal waters in the Gulf of Mexico. To prevent federal authorities from confirming that he had harvested undersized fish, Yates ordered a crew member to toss the suspect catch into the sea. For this offense, he was charged with, and convicted of, violating 18 U.S.C. §1519, which provides:

FACTS

PROCEDURAL LAW

> "Whoever knowingly alters, destroys, mutilates, conceals, covers up, falsifies, or makes a false entry in any record, document, or tangible object

SUBSTANTIVE LAW (Statute)

2. When no single opinion gains the support of a majority of the court (at least 5 for the U.S. Supreme Court), the opinion that has the most support is issued as a plurality opinion.

> with the intent to impede, obstruct, or influence the investigation or proper administration of any matter within the jurisdiction of any department or agency of the United States or any case filed under title 11, or in relation to or contemplation of any such matter or case, shall be fined under this title, imprisoned not more than 20 years, or both."

PARTY ARGUMENT

Yates . . . maintains that fish are not trapped within the term "tangible object," as that term is used in §1519.

SUBSTANTIVE LAW (Meaning of statute)

Section 1519 was enacted as part of the Sarbanes-Oxley Act of 2002, legislation designed to protect investors and restore trust in financial markets following the collapse of Enron Corporation. A fish is no doubt an object that is tangible; fish can be seen, caught, and handled, and a catch, as this case illustrates, is vulnerable to destruction. But it would cut §1519 loose from its financial-fraud mooring to hold that it encompasses any and all objects, whatever their size or significance, destroyed with obstructive intent. Mindful that in Sarbanes-Oxley, Congress trained its attention on corporate and accounting deception and cover-ups, we conclude that a matching construction of §1519 is in order: A tangible object captured by §1519, we hold, must be one used to record or preserve information.

SUBSTANTIVE LAW (Holding)

I

FACTS

On August 23, 2007, the *Miss Katie,* a commercial fishing boat, was six days into an expedition in the Gulf of Mexico. Her crew numbered three, including Yates, the captain. Engaged in a routine offshore patrol to inspect both recreational and commercial vessels, Officer John Jones of the Florida Fish and Wildlife Conservation Commission decided to board the *Miss Katie* to check on the vessel's compliance with fishing rules . . . .

Upon boarding the *Miss Katie,* Officer Jones noticed three red grouper that appeared to be undersized hanging from a hook on the deck. At the time, federal conservation regulations required immediate release of red grouper less than 20 inches long . . . .

Suspecting that other undersized fish might be on board, Officer Jones proceeded to inspect the ship's catch, setting aside and measuring only fish that appeared to him to be shorter than 20 inches. Officer Jones ultimately determined that 72 fish fell short of the 20-inch mark. A fellow officer recorded the length of each of the undersized fish on a catch measurement verification form. With few exceptions, the measured fish were between 19 and 20 inches; three were less than 19 inches; none were less than 18.75 inches. After separating the fish measuring below 20 inches from the rest of the catch by placing them in wooden crates, Officer Jones directed Yates to leave the fish, thus segregated, in the crates until the *Miss Katie* returned to port. Before departing, Officer Jones issued Yates a citation for possession of undersized fish.

Four days later, after the *Miss Katie* had docked in Cortez, Florida, Officer Jones measured the fish contained in the wooden crates. This time, however, the measured fish, although still less than 20 inches, slightly exceeded the lengths recorded on board. Jones surmised that the fish brought to port were not the same as those he had detected during his initial inspection. Under questioning, one of the crew members admitted that, at Yates's direction, he had thrown overboard the fish Officer Jones had measured at sea, and that he and Yates had replaced the tossed grouper with fish from the rest of the catch.

PROCEDURAL POSTURE

For reasons not disclosed in the record before us, more than 32 months passed before criminal charges were lodged against Yates. On May 5, 2010, he was indicted for . . . destroying, concealing, and covering up undersized fish to impede a federal investigation, in violation of §1519. By the time of the indictment, the minimum legal length for Gulf red grouper had been lowered from 20 inches to 18 inches. No measured fish in Yates's catch fell below that limit. The record does not reveal what civil penalty, if any, Yates received for his possession of fish undersized under the 2007 regulation.

Yates was tried on the criminal charges in August 2011. At the end of the Government's case in chief, he moved for a judgment of acquittal on the §1519 charge. Pointing to §1519's title and its origin as a provision of the Sarbanes-Oxley Act, Yates argued that the section sets forth "a documents offense" and that its reference to "tangible object[s]" subsumes "computer hard drives, logbooks, [and] things of that nature," not fish . . . .

The Government countered that a "tangible object" within §1519's compass is "simply something other than a document or record." . . . [T]he trial court read "tangible object" as a term "independent" of "record" or "document." For violating §1519 . . . the court sentenced Yates to imprisonment for 30 days, followed by supervised release for three years. For life, he will bear the stigma of having a federal felony conviction.

On appeal, the Eleventh Circuit found the text of §1519 "plain." Because "tangible object" was "undefined" in the statutes, the Court of Appeals gave the term its "ordinary or natural meaning," *i.e.* its dictionary definition, "[h]aving or possessing physical form."

HOLDING

We . . . now reverse the Eleventh Circuit's judgment.

II

PARTY ARGUMENTS

The Sarbanes-Oxley Act, all agree, was prompted by the exposure of Enron's massive accounting fraud and revelations that the company's outside auditor, Arthur Andersen LLP, had systematically destroyed potentially incriminating documents. The Government acknowledges that §1519 was intended to prohibit, in particular, corporate document-shredding to hide evidence of financial wrongdoing . . . .

In the Government's view, §1519 extends beyond the principal evil motivating its passage. The words of §1519, the Government argues, support reading the provision as a general ban on the spoliation of evidence, covering all physical items that might be relevant to any matter under federal investigation.

Yates urges a contextual reading of §1519, tying "tangible object" to the surrounding words, the placement of the provision within the Sarbanes-Oxley Act, and related provisions enacted at the same time . . . . Section 1519, he maintains, targets not all manner of evidence, but records, documents, and tangible objects used to preserve them, *e.g.,* computers, servers, and other media on which information is stored.

HOLDING

We agree with Yates and reject the Government's unrestrained reading. "Tangible object" in §1519, we conclude, is better read to cover only objects one can use to record or preserve information, not all objects in the physical world.

A

REASONING

The ordinary meaning of an "object" that is "tangible," as stated in dictionary definitions, is "a discrete . . . thing," Webster's Third New International Dictionary 1555 (2002), that "possess[es] physical form," Black's Law Dictionary 1683 (10th ed. 2014). From this premise, the Government concludes that "tangible object," as that term appears in §1519, covers the waterfront, including fish from the sea.

LEGAL PRINCIPLE: Words can be ambiguous even if their dictionary definitions are clear

Whether a statutory term is unambiguous, however, does not turn solely on dictionary definitions of its component words. Rather, "[t]he plainness or ambiguity of statutory language is determined [not only] by reference to the language itself, [but as well by] the specific context in which that language is used, and the broader context of the statute as a whole." . . . Ordinarily, a word's usage accords with its dictionary definition. In law as in life, however, the same words, placed in different contexts, sometimes mean different things . . . .

In short, although dictionary definitions of the words "tangible" and "object" bear consideration, they are not dispositive of the meaning of "tangible object" in §1519 . . . .

B

Familiar interpretive guides aid our construction of the words "tangible object" as they appear in §1519.

We note first §1519's caption: "Destruction, alteration, or falsification of records in Federal investigations

LEGAL PRINCIPLE: Headings help to interpret words in statutes

UNDERLYING LEGAL PRINCIPLE: Congress's intent matters in interpreting a statute

LEGAL PRINCIPLE: Surrounding words help to interpret words in statutes

HOLDING

and bankruptcy." That heading conveys no suggestion that the section prohibits spoliation of any and all physical evidence, however remote from records. Neither does the title of the section of the Sarbanes-Oxley Act in which §1519 was placed: "Criminal penalties for altering documents." . . . While these headings are not commanding, they supply cues that Congress did not intend "tangible object" in §1519 to sweep within its reach physical objects of every kind, including things no one would describe as records, documents, or devices closely associated with them . . . . If Congress indeed meant to make §1519 an all-encompassing ban on the spoliation of evidence, as the dissent believes Congress did, one would have expected a clearer indication of that intent . . . .

The words immediately surrounding "tangible object" in §1519—"falsifies, or makes a false entry in any record [or] document"—also cabin the contextual meaning of that term . . . ." Tangible object" is the last in a list of terms that begins "any record [or] document." The term is therefore appropriately read to refer, not to any tangible object, but specifically to the subset of tangible objects involving records and documents, *i.e.,* objects used to record or preserve information.

This moderate interpretation of "tangible object" accords with the list of actions §1519 proscribes. The section applies to anyone who "alters, destroys, mutilates, conceals, covers up, *falsifies,* or *makes a false entry in* any record, document, or tangible object" with the requisite obstructive intent. (Emphasis added.) The last two verbs, "falsif[y]" and "mak[e] a false entry in," typically take as grammatical objects records, documents, or things used to record or preserve information, such as logbooks or hard drives . . . . It would be unnatural, for example, to describe a killer's act of wiping his fingerprints from a gun as "falsifying" the murder weapon. But it would not be strange to refer to "falsifying" data stored on a hard drive as simply "falsifying" a hard drive . . . .

Having used traditional tools of statutory interpretation to examine markers of congressional intent within the Sarbanes-Oxley Act and §1519 itself, we are persuaded that an aggressive interpretation of "tangible object" must be rejected. It is highly improbable that Congress would have buried a general spoliation statute covering objects of any and every kind in a provision targeting fraud in financial record-keeping . . . .

C

Finally, if our recourse to traditional tools of statutory construction leaves any doubt about the meaning of "tangible object," as that term is used in §1519, we would invoke the rule that "ambiguity concerning the ambit of criminal statutes should be resolved in favor of lenity." . . .

LEGAL PRINCIPLE: Interpret criminal laws leniently

For the reasons stated, we resist reading §1519 expansively to create a coverall spoliation of evidence statute, advisable as such a measure might be. Leaving that important decision to Congress, we hold that a "tangible object" within §1519's compass is one used to record or preserve information. The judgment of the U.S. Court of Appeals for the Eleventh Circuit is therefore reversed, and the case is remanded for further proceedings.

HOLDING

It is so ordered.

OPINION CONCURRING IN JUDGMENT[3]

Justice Alito, concurring in the judgment.

This case can and should be resolved on narrow grounds. And though the question is close, traditional tools of statutory construction confirm that John Yates has the better of the argument. Three features of 18 U.S.C. §1519 stand out to me: the statute's list of nouns, its list of verbs, and its title. Although perhaps none of these features by itself would tip the case in favor of Yates, the three combined do so.

LEGAL PRINCIPLE: Decide cases on narrow grounds

Start with the nouns. Section 1519 refers to "any record, document, or tangible object." . . . [T]he term "tangible object" should refer to something similar

REASONING

3. An opinion concurring in judgment disagrees with the majority's (or plurality's, as here) reasoning but agrees with the outcome.

LEGAL PRINCIPLE: Surrounding words help to interpret words in statutes

to records or documents. A fish does not spring to mind—nor does an antelope, a colonial farmhouse, a hydrofoil, or an oil derrick. All are "objects" that are "tangible." But who wouldn't raise an eyebrow if a neighbor, when asked to identify something similar to a "record" or "document," said "crocodile"? . . .

Next, consider §1519's list of verbs: "alters, destroys, mutilates, conceals, covers up, falsifies, or makes a false entry in." Although many of those verbs could apply to nouns as far-flung as salamanders, satellites, or sand dunes, the last phrase in the list—"makes a false entry in"—makes no sense outside of filekeeping. How does one make a false entry in a fish? . . .

LEGAL PRINCIPLE: Titles help to interpret words in statutes

Finally, my analysis is influenced by §1519's title: "Destruction, alteration, or falsification of *records* in Federal investigations and bankruptcy." (Emphasis added.) This too points toward filekeeping, not fish. Titles can be useful devices to resolve "'doubt about the meaning of a statute.'" The title is especially valuable here because it reinforces what the text's nouns and verbs independently suggest—that no matter how other statutes might be read, this particular one does not cover every noun in the universe with tangible form.

DISSENTING OPINION[4]

Justice Kagan, with whom Justice Scalia, Justice Kennedy, and Justice Thomas join, dissenting.

A criminal law, 18 U.S.C. §1519, prohibits tampering with "any record, document, or tangible object" in an attempt to obstruct a federal investigation. This case raises the question whether the term "tangible object" means the same thing in §1519 as it means in everyday language—any object capable of being touched. The answer should be easy: Yes. The term "tangible object" is broad, but clear. Throughout the U.S. Code and many States' laws, it invariably covers physical objects of all kinds. And in §1519, context confirms what bare text says: All the words surrounding "tangible object" show that Congress meant the

REASONING

term to have a wide range. That fits with Congress's evident purpose in enacting §1519: to punish those who alter or destroy physical evidence—*any* physical evidence—with the intent of thwarting federal law enforcement.

The plurality instead interprets "tangible object" to cover "only objects one can use to record or preserve information." The concurring opinion similarly, if more vaguely, contends that "tangible object" should refer to "something similar to records or documents"—and shouldn't include colonial farmhouses, crocodiles, or fish. In my view, conventional tools of statutory construction all lead to a more conventional result: A "tangible object" is an object that's tangible. I would apply the statute that Congress enacted and affirm the judgment below.

LEGAL PRINCIPLE: words should be given their conventional meanings

I

While the plurality starts its analysis with §1519's heading, I would begin with §1519's text. When Congress has not supplied a definition, we generally give a statutory term its ordinary meaning. As the plurality must acknowledge, the ordinary meaning of "tangible object" is "a discrete thing that possesses physical form." A fish is, of course, a discrete thing that possesses physical form. See generally Dr. Seuss, One Fish Two Fish Red Fish Blue Fish (1960). So the ordinary meaning of the term "tangible object" in §1519, as no one here disputes, covers fish (including too-small red grouper).

LEGAL PRINCIPLE: statutory interpretation starts with the text of the statute

That interpretation accords with endless uses of the term in statute and rule books as construed by courts. Dozens of federal laws and rules of procedure (and hundreds of state enactments) include the term "tangible object" or its first cousin "tangible thing"—some in association with documents, others not . . . .

As Congress recognized in using a broad term, giving immunity to those who destroy non-documentary evidence has no sensible basis in penal policy. A person

LEGAL PRINCIPLE: interpret a word in one statute by comparing it to the same word in other statutes who hides a murder victim's body is no less culpable than one who burns the victim's diary. A fisherman, like John Yates, who dumps undersized fish to avoid a fine is no less blameworthy than one who shreds his vessel's catch log for the same reason. Congress thus treated both offenders in the same way. It understood, in enacting §1519, that destroying evidence is destroying evidence, whether or not that evidence takes documentary form . . . .

The concurring opinion is a shorter, vaguer version of the plurality's . . . .

But §1519's meaning should not hinge on the odd game of Mad Libs the concurrence proposes. No one reading §1519 needs to fill in a blank after the words "records" and "documents." That is because Congress, quite helpfully, already did so—adding the term "tangible object." The issue in this case is what that term means. So if the concurrence wishes to ask its neighbor a question, I'd recommend a more pertinent one: Do you think a fish (or, if the concurrence prefers, a crocodile) is a "tangible object"? As to that query, "who wouldn't raise an eyebrow" if the neighbor said "no"? . . .

I respectfully dissent.

Here is what your finished brief might look like:

- **Facts.** Yates ordered undersized fish thrown overboard between the time he was first caught with them and the time he returned to the dock.
- **Procedural posture.** Yates was charged with violating §1519 for destroying a tangible object. He argued in the trial court that the statute did not cover destroying fish, but both the district court and the Court of Appeals rejected that argument. He was therefore convicted, and his conviction was upheld by the Court of Appeals.
- **Holding.** A four-Justice plurality joined by Justice Alito in a separate opinion held that a fish is not a tangible object for purposes of §1519.

- Reasoning. Both the majority and Justice Alito use traditional tools of statutory interpretation to suggest that Congress did not mean to include "fish" in the term "tangible object" in §1519, but that it is instead limited to things like records and documents. The dissenting Justices focus on the plain meaning of the words "tangible object."

You're not done with your second reading. You still need to extract the legal principles. Justice Ginsburg's plurality opinion relies on five basic legal principles:

- Words can be ambiguous even if their dictionary definitions are clear. That's why a "tangible object" is not necessarily (as Justice Kagan describes it) "an object that's tangible."
- Congress's intent matters in interpreting a statute. Notice that this is slightly out of order, and that it is marked as an "underlying" legal principle. The plurality opinion doesn't come right out and say that Congress's intent matters. Instead the plurality rests its conclusion about the meaning of the statute in part on the fact that Congress intended one thing rather than another. That must mean these Justices think Congress's intent should be relevant to the interpretation of statutes. You will need to be able to identify these hidden sorts of principles in cases.
- Headings help to interpret words in statutes.
- Surrounding words help to interpret words in statutes.
- Criminal laws should be interpreted leniently.

Know these principles and have them handy. Your professor is sure to ask about them in class.

Your professor also will ask you about the additional opinions since they have been included in your casebook. The questions will focus on comparing and contrasting the concurring or dissenting opinions to the plurality opinion (or to each other). What are the real differences between the opinions? Why did the author of a separate opinion choose certain legal principles to the exclusion of others?

Justice Alito's concurrence agrees with the outcome but also agrees with some of the plurality's reasoning. Alito agrees that surrounding words matter, and he argues that the title, like the heading, helps interpret words in statutes. But, since he wrote separately, he disagrees with at least one legal principle in the majority opinion. You can rule out the first principle because if he thought that the phrase "tangible object" unambiguously meant its dictionary definition, he would have agreed with the dissent. He must think either that Congress's intent shouldn't matter in interpreting a statute or that criminal laws need not be interpreted leniently. The reason (or reasons) for his refusal to join the plurality is very likely to come up in class.

Justice Kagan's dissent, of course, states its own legal principles. She contends that words should be given their conventional meanings. Statutory interpretation starts with the text of the statute. Finally, courts should interpret a word in one statute by comparing it to the same word in other statutes. These principles lead her to reach a conclusion opposite that reached by the majority.

Test Your Understanding

Joshua builds a fence on what he thinks is his property. Hannah, his neighbor, believes that the fence is on her property. Hannah hires a surveyor, who confirms that it is on her property, but Joshua refuses to take it down. Hannah sues Joshua, seeking an injunction requiring the removal of the fence and damages to compensate Hannah for the cost of hiring the surveyor.

The trial court issues the following opinion:

1. If a property owner does not object to another's known trespass on her property, the owner is deemed to have consented to the trespass.
2. Joshua asked Hannah about building the fence, and Hannah did not object.
3. Therefore, Hannah consented to the fence.

Judgment is issued in favor of Joshua; no relief is granted to Hannah. Hannah appeals, and the court of appeals affirms (that is, agrees with) the trial court.

Which parts of this account are procedural, and which are substantive? Which parts of the trial court's opinion are about questions of fact? Which are about questions of law? And which apply the law to the facts? What is the relevant legal principle?

Step Three: Evaluate the Reasoning

So far, your reading has been all about the case. What does it say? What does it do? What does it mean? Now, on your third reading, you must think critically about the material. One way to think critically is to determine whether you agree with the principles announced. For example, think about the difference between the plurality and the dissent on how best to interpret a statute. The plurality focuses on what Congress intended the words to mean, while the dissent (and possibly Justice Alito) focuses instead on the plain meaning of the words in the text. Which is a better approach, and why?

More importantly, however, you need to evaluate the opinion on its own terms. Does what the court says make sense to you? Is the opinion internally consistent? Do the conclusions follow from the premises? To answer these questions, you have to understand styles of legal reasoning. Lawyers use two basic types of reasoning: **analytical** (also called vertical) and **analogical** (also called horizontal).

Analytical Reasoning. Analytical reasoning can be deductive or inductive. Both involve the relationship between the general and the particular, which is why both types are often called "vertical" reasoning. But they move in opposite directions. Deductive analytical reasoning starts with general, universally applicable statements and deduces particular conclusions. Inductive analytical reasoning starts with many particular factual statements and uses them to create a generalized conclusion. Thus, both inductive and deductive reasoning involve universal statements, but with an important difference: the universal is a premise in deductive reasoning and a conclusion in inductive reasoning. In this section we will start by illustrating deductive reasoning and then turn to inductive reasoning.

Deductive analytical reasoning is deductive because the argument deduces a conclusion from two (or more) premises (the LSAT tests deductive analytical reasoning in the logical reasoning section). The outcome is dictated by the starting principles, moving from general to particular. You can better understand this concept through examples of logical arguments (often called "syllogisms"). We'll start with this famous example involving the mortality of Socrates.

Socrates Is Mortal (Sound Argument)

Premise 1: All men are mortal.
Premise 2: Socrates is a man.
Conclusion: Socrates is mortal.

This seems simple enough. Yet deductive reasoning is often misused. You should watch out for common errors. For example, premises and conclusions may be mistakenly switched as they are in the next two examples.

All Men Are Mortal (Switched Premise/Conclusion)

Premise 1: Socrates is a man.
Premise 2: Socrates is mortal.
Conclusion: All men are mortal.

If all men are mortal, then we can logically conclude that this man (Socrates) must be mortal. But just because one man (Socrates) is mortal does not logically require that all men are mortal. The premises do not support the conclusion. The conclusion's truth is not proven by this argument. Thus, this is not sound reasoning (even though we know the conclusion to be true).

Socrates Is a Man (Switched Premise/Conclusion)

Premise 1: All men are mortal.
Premise 2: Socrates is mortal.
Conclusion: Socrates is a man.

Again, just because Socrates and men are mortal does not necessarily prove that Socrates is a man. He was in fact a man, but this argument does not prove it. Thus, unsound reasoning does not mean that the conclusion is false.

Test Your Understanding

Evaluate the soundness of this deductive analytic argument:

Premise 1: A valid contract requires consideration.
Premise 2: There is consideration for this contract.
Conclusion: This is a valid contract.

Another potential problem is that deductive reasoning may be used implicitly such that a premise or the conclusion are missing (or hidden). Consider the assertion that "because Socrates is a man, he must be mortal." How do you evaluate the soundness of this statement? You can begin by turning the statement into a logical argument that is missing a premise:

Is Socrates Mortal? (Missing Premise)

Premise 1: Socrates is a man.
Premise 2:?
Conclusion: Socrates is mortal.

This allows you to see that the missing premise is that all men are mortal. Now you can evaluate the argument by testing the premises.

You can see how hidden premises work by looking again at the plurality opinion in *Yates*. After suggesting that the headings in §1519 seem to refer mostly to documents and similar objects, the opinion states: "If Congress indeed meant to make §1519 an all-encompassing ban on the spoliation of evidence, as the dissent believes Congress did, one would have expected a clearer indication of that intent." The opinion ultimately concludes that "tangible objects" do not include fish. You can turn this reasoning into a logical argument:

Yates Syllogism (Hidden Premise)

Premise 1: Congress did not intend "tangible object" to include fish (we know that from the headings and the surrounding words).
Premise 2:?
Conclusion: "Tangible object" does not include fish.

The missing premise is the one we identified as an underlying legal principle: Congress's intent matters in interpreting a statute. Now you can evaluate the syllogism, and conclude that *if* the premises are correct, the conclusion does indeed follow.

Deductive reasoning requires that all of the premises be true. One common problem is that one of the premises of a logical argument is false. For example, if Socrates is not a man or if not all men are mortal, the "Socrates Is Mortal" argument is logically sound, but the conclusion is nevertheless unsound. Thus, one way to attack a conclusion is to question the validity of the premises.

A close look at the premises may reveal that one of the premises is itself a conclusion from an earlier syllogism. Imagine trying to break down the first premise from the Socrates Is a Man example. You may find that the premise is proven through an earlier argument.

Socrates the Philosopher Is a Man (Proving a Premise)

Premise 1: Socrates wrote philosophy.
Premise 2: Only men write philosophy.
Conclusion: Socrates is a man.

Socrates Is Mortal (Premise Is Prior Conclusion)

Premise 1: Socrates is a man.
Premise 2: All men are mortal.
Conclusion: Socrates is mortal.

The conclusion in the first argument becomes the first premise of the second argument. Complex arguments, like those in judicial opinions, are often constructed in this way. Judges, however, rarely make the connections so clear. You will need to break down the arguments in order to see the necessary steps to the court's conclusion.

Test Your Understanding

Create a new deductive-analytical argument based on factually accurate premises that supports Premise 1 of the following syllogism:

Premise 1: All law students have taken at least one multiple choice test before law school.
Premise 2: Some law school tests are multiple choice.
Conclusion: Not all law school tests will be new to law students.

There is one other twist to the examination of the premises: You have to be careful about definitions. Note the second premise of Socrates the Philosopher Is a Man: "Only men write philosophy." If "men" means male humans, then the premise is obviously false because we can immediately provide counter-examples. But if we are using the word "men" in its more inclusive sense, to mean all humans, it seems to be true (at least we can't think of any counter-examples!). When comparing judicial opinions that reach opposite conclusions, you should look for different starting premises as well as different definitions in the same starting premise.

Deductive reasoning, when done correctly, is the most powerful form of argument because the conclusion is logically compelled. Always read or listen for deductive arguments (and then try to pick holes in them). And always try, if you can, to structure your own arguments in deductive analytical form.

Inductive analytical reasoning, like deductive reasoning, also works vertically, but it is bottom-up rather than top-down. While deductive reasoning uses general statements to draw a specific conclusion, inductive reasoning uses particular statements to draw a general conclusion.

You might have noticed that none of the examples above prove that all men are mortal. Suppose that instead of starting with the *premise* that all men are mortal, we are trying to *prove* that all men are mortal. Universal mortality, in other words, is a conclusion rather than a premise. Suppose an adversary challenges the validity of this premise. How can we prove that all men are mortal? We will have to use inductive reasoning, using known specifics to argue the validity of our (as yet unproven) general conclusion:

All Men Are Mortal (Proof by Induction)

Specific Statement 1: Socrates was a man, and he was mortal.
Specific Statement 2: Plato was a man, and he was mortal.
Specific Statement 3: Aristotle was a man, and he was mortal.
Specific Statements 4 and up: [Fill in the blank] was a man, and he was mortal.
Conclusion: All men are mortal.

Inductive reasoning requires us to collect enough examples of mortal men (and to discover no examples of immortal men!) to allow us to conclude more-or-less confidently that "all men are mortal." Notice that we say "more-or-less confidently": one important difference between deductive and inductive reasoning is that deductive reasoning—if used correctly—can logically prove a conclusion, while inductive reasoning cannot. The most we can do with inductive reasoning is build a higher and higher level of confidence in the truth of our general conclusion.

As with deductive reasoning, there are several common ways that inductive reasoning can go wrong. One common mistake is to draw inferences from too few cases. If you've taken an undergraduate course in logic, you will recognize this mistake as a logical fallacy called a "hasty generalization." If you know the lifespans of only five people, you cannot draw any valid inferences about the human lifespan. An inference from such a limited sample size would be a hasty generalization. Another common mistake is to base a generalization on cases that are not sufficiently similar to the matter at hand to have inferential value. Information regarding the lifespans of elephants or fruit flies cannot support a generalization about the human lifespan.

Analogical Reasoning. Analogical reasoning, or reasoning by analogy, draws arguments from across parallel cases rather than from first premises to reach a conclusion as to a specific analogous case. That's why it is sometimes called "horizontal" reasoning. It does not rely on or produce universal or generally applicable statements the way that analytical reasoning does.

Lionel Messi Is Mortal

Specific Statement 1: Socrates was a man, and he was mortal.
Specific Statement 2: Plato was a man, and he was mortal.
Specific Statement 3: Aristotle was a man, and he was mortal.
Specific Conclusion: Lionel Messi is a man, and he is therefore mortal.

Analogical reasoning, unlike inductive analytical reasoning, does not take the additional step of concluding that *all* men are mortal.

Like inductive reasoning, analogical reasoning can create only a greater or lesser degree of confidence; unlike deductive reasoning, it cannot definitively prove the conclusion. (In our example, if we continued the list of specific statements to include hundreds of mortals, we would have a very high degree of confidence.) Similarly, analogical reasoning can suffer from the same flaws as other forms of inductive reasoning: if you use too few specific cases, or the wrong cases, your conclusion might be unjustified.

Effective analogical reasoning draws the *right* analogies. Are the prior cases on which you rely similar enough to draw an inference applicable to the current case? You need to learn how to identify which cases are relevant and to assess how many cases are needed to establish a principle. In order to decide whether a particular analogy is apt, you have to be able to determine which legal or factual differences are significant (and which are not).

In the Lionel Messi Is Mortal example, we drew an analogy based on three specific statements. All three statements were about ancient Greek philosophers. May we only draw an analogy from those statements to other ancient Greek philosophers? Is the time when they lived, their nationality, and/or their occupation relevant to their mortality? If so, then we cannot draw an analogy to evaluate whether Lionel Messi, a contemporary international football star, is mortal. If those characteristics are not relevant but the fact that they were human is, then we can draw the analogy.

One important skill for legal reasoning, then, is being able to pick out *relevant* similarities and differences. Let's try another example.

Imagine a statute that imposes a higher tax on imported "dolls" than on imported "action figures." Would the higher tax apply to a 12-inch Mickey Mouse toy with a soft (stuffed) body and movable plastic arms, legs, and head? Your client wants to know because the tax affects pricing the toy. Your research uncovers the following cases applying the statute:

- A soft plush princess named Elsa (from the Frozen stories) is a doll.
- An all-plastic soldier named G.I. Joe is an action figure.
- An all-plastic baby named Enrique is a doll.
- A set of bendable plastic superheroes is a set of action figures.
- A silicone figure named Elsa (the same character in a different material), which looks like the actress who played the part in the movies and comes with a display stand, is a doll.

Two possible inferences might jump out at you: all the dolls (and none of the action figures) have names that begin with E, and both forms of the Elsa toys from the Frozen movies are dolls. But are these significant distinctions? How likely is it that the legislators enacting the tariffs, or the courts applying the tariff statute, meant to draw a distinction based on either? Not very.

A closer examination reveals two other possible distinguishing features. Children play differently with action figures, giving the toys more active roles than dolls, which are assigned more passive parts. Dolls also appear to be more likely to be categorized as "girl" toys and action figures are often deemed "boy" toys. Where does that leave the Frozen toy? If it is marketed to boys, you could argue that it should be an action figure. But, again, is it likely that the legislature created two categories based merely on gender stereotypes? Alternatively, you could argue that the movable parts mean that the toy will be given an active part in imaginary games and thus is an action figure.

This example illustrates several things about analogical reasoning. First, unlike deductive reasoning, it often fails to produce just one unequivocally right answer (law is often uncertain, as we've seen before and will see again). Second, reasoning by analogy—unlike deductive reasoning—is concrete and contextual rather than abstract. It *matters* that legislators are more likely to care about how the toys will be used than about whether their names begin with E.

While it is easier to reason by analogy from many prior cases, you may have only one prior case on which to rely (or cases which only come out one way). The basic principle is the same: identify the relevant factors on which to compare your case to the known case. Your prior experience should give you some basis for figuring out which factors are relevant and which are irrelevant. Time in the law school classroom will sharpen your skills.

After you evaluate the reasoning used in the opinion, you must *elaborate* on it. You should try to predict where courts will go next, based on the reasoning in the case or cases you are reading. That will require you to use primarily analogical reasoning. The cases you are reading are like the list of previously decided tariff cases, and you must invent and decide new cases like the one about the Harry Potter toy. Come up with hypotheticals by using your imagination, discussing the case with classmates, and looking through the notes in the casebook. Indeed, much of your time in classes and in your legal writing assignments will require applying rules from previous cases to new sets of facts—in other words, using analogical reasoning to analogize and distinguish cases.

Test Your Understanding

Go back to *Yates* and consider some possible implications of the plurality's reasoning. Does §1519 cover:

1. Deleting e-mails related to financial fraud?
2. Deleting Facebook posts related to financial fraud?
3. Sending information related to financial fraud via Snapchat so it will automatically disappear?
4. Destroying physical records unrelated to financial fraud?
5. Filing off the serial number from a gun so that it can't be identified when it is used in a crime? What about if the crime is bank robbery?
6. Destroying a ledger that has on it blood evidence from a murder?

READING AND WRITING LIKE A LAWYER: PREPARING FOR CLASS

To prepare well for class, it is not enough to read like a lawyer. Effective class preparation requires active reading and active writing. You should write two things: annotations in the casebook itself and a separate brief. And remember: don't take shortcuts! It can be very tempting to read case briefs written by someone else or to skim the material, especially later in the semester when you are busy and more confident. But your understanding of the material—and, ultimately, your performance on the final exam—will suffer if you do not do the work yourself.

Briefing is easy to explain but hard to do. Reading this book will give you a big head start on the path to mastering briefing. You begin by writing out the facts, procedural posture, holding, and reasoning in your own words. Quote only the most significant language—the language that you will use to explain the implications and application of the case. The rest should be in your own words. Revise how you brief as the semester unfolds. Adapt to your professor and to the subject. Over time, your briefs will get shorter, and you'll be able to rely more heavily on what you write directly in your casebook.

Annotating the reading is as important as briefing. Underline, highlight, or circle important language or key principles. Put a star or an exclamation point or some other signal in the margin next to significant passages. Have a system: maybe two stars are more important than one star, which is more important than just an exclamation point. Try to peek at your professor's book in class—we are sure that you will see it is covered with these types of notes (even when the professor wrote the book!).

Write *words* in the margin: signals of what is happening in the text. Look again at our mark-up of *Yates* for ideas. Use anything that seems comfortable to you and appropriate to the particular cases. If the opinion states a particular test, you might mark that passage "TEST." If the court had distinguished precedent—and actually it did, but we edited that out—mark it as "PRECEDENT DISTINGUISHED."

You have to be judicious in highlighting or underlining. Instead of underlining a whole sentence, underline only a few key words that will help you remember what the sentence is about when you reread it. Here is one way to underline the text in *Yates*:

> The <u>words immediately surrounding</u> "tangible object" in §1519—"falsifies, or makes a false entry in any record [or] document"—also <u>cabin</u> the contextual <u>meaning</u> of that term . . . . "<u>Tangible object</u>" is the <u>last in a list</u> of terms that <u>begins</u> "<u>any record [or] document</u>." The term is therefore appropriately read to refer, not to any tangible object, but specifically to the <u>subset of tangible objects involving records and documents</u>, *i.e.*, objects used to record or preserve information.

Remember, you should still note in the margin that this passage states the legal principle that surrounding words help interpret a term in a statute. The underlining just helps you fill in the details of how the court applies that principle in this case.

How do you know what to highlight? Think about what you will need if you have to find answers quickly. The excerpted paragraph above defines "tangible object," and the important considerations are that the phrase appears in a list of items that are similar or related in particular ways. When your professor asks you *why* the plurality concluded that a fish is not a tangible object, our suggested underlining makes the relevant considerations stand out. Your annotations serve as signals about what you found important. Done correctly, you can read just the underlining and will get a relatively coherent account by inserting your own short connectors in your head: "Words immediately surrounding [a word] cabin [its] meaning. Tangible object [is] last in a list [that] begins 'any record or document' [and therefore refers to the] subset of tangible objects involving records and documents."

You should also annotate statutes, rules, and regulations. In a statute, a single word may make all the difference. It matters tremendously whether a statute uses "and" or "or," whether it says a person "shall" do something or "may" do something, or whether an obligation is imposed "if" something occurs or "unless" it occurs. Look for—and highlight—operative but easy-to-miss words like that in addition to the more obvious nouns and verbs.

Everyone develops a system and a style of learning in law school. You don't need to completely depart from the ways you've learned in the past, but you should recognize that this is new territory. The first year—and especially the first semester—is all about developing skills, methods, and routines that will help you succeed. And the need to develop those skills, methods, and routines is yet another reason to avoid shortcuts like study aids!

READING AND WRITING LIKE A LAWYER: IN CLASS

Your focus on language does not end when you have finished preparing for class. You need to think carefully about language *in* class as well.

Our advice on taking notes can be summarized in one sentence: don't try to take verbatim notes! You are not a speech recognition program converting speech to text.

To benefit from class, you need to listen, think, and participate. You can't do that if you're trying desperately to type every word the professor says. One caveat: if the professor simply lectures, rather than using the Socratic method described in Chapter 1, then it's OK to write down as much as you possibly can. But be sure to go over it later and think about it in the way we will recommend for Socratic classes.

Your class notes should be judicious. Choose carefully both what to write down and exactly how to write it. If you have prepared well for class, at least some of what happens in class will not be a surprise to you. And you will *already* have written—in your brief or in the casebook margins—much of what is said. Listen carefully to both the professor and your classmates, and as they speak, you should be mentally comparing what they say with what you already think you know. When the two match up, just put a check mark next to your own brief or annotation—you got that one right and there's no need to do anything more than confirm it. This is one advantage of writing in advance of class: it means less need to write during class.

Your brief or annotations may be right but still not match class discussion. If the student reciting the facts of the *Yates* case talks about "grouper" rather than "fish," or gives more specific information about the people, events, or timing than you have in your brief, think about whether those details are important. Remember: you already made the decision once to leave out that information. Just because another student puts it in—and the professor seems happy with that student or writes the information on the board—does not mean you were wrong. Try to figure out, as the discussion proceeds, whether it is important that the fish happened to be grouper or that the official was a member of the Florida Fish and Wildlife Conservation Commission.

Sometimes, however much you have prepared for class, the discussion will turn to aspects of the assigned material that you overlooked or misunderstood (if it didn't, the professor would be out of a job!). You will need to write down just enough that you will be able to reconstruct the new ideas after class. Focus on *listening* to what's being said and *understanding* it, not on writing it down.

Remember to write in your own words as much as possible. Translating what the professor (or a classmate) says into your own words helps you understand it and remember it. You have to think about and evaluate what they are saying. Maybe you disagree with it, maybe you think it should be tweaked or refined in some way. Make a note of your thoughts.

If you follow our advice, when you walk out of class each day you won't have much in your notes. That means it is very important to *reconstruct* the larger class discussion from what little you have. As soon after class as you can, go through your class notes and annotate and amplify them. Take the hints and reminders you have written to yourself and turn them into something that looks more like a summary of the take-away points of the class. You can do this by expanding your notes, or by making additional annotations to your brief or your marginal comments, or both. Some students find it helpful to review the class with other students because each student might have a slightly different set of in-class notes.

Taking notes this way is almost certainly new to you and will take some practice. The basic idea is to: (1) set yourself up by preparing well, (2) take as few notes as possible so you can actually process what's happening in class instead of writing, and (3) flesh out your notes while the class itself is still fresh in your memory. Be comforted by the knowledge that all of your classmates are in the same boat—and for that reason, professors will start out slowly, will often repeat or summarize material over consecutive classes, and will not expect you to remember everything immediately.

COMMUNICATING LIKE A LAWYER

Everything we have said so far involves the way you use language to learn the law. But in law school—and life as a lawyer—you will also have to use language carefully and precisely in order to communicate what you know. The same basic rules apply: pay attention to each word, be precise rather than vague, speak in specifics not generalities, and cull irrelevancies and redundancies.

When you are answering a question in class, you will already have a head start if you have followed our techniques. You will have briefed the case and made notes about the legal principles, problems, and implications of the case. Your casebook annotations will make it easy to find the passages in the case that respond to the professor's question or support your answer. You can concentrate on how to articulate your response to the question. The same is true of writing assignments and exams. If you have prepared well, you will have the knowledge you need and can focus on how best to answer the question.

The same rules apply to both in-class questions and written assignments (including exams). Be *organized, precise,* and *concise.*

Be Organized. Listen carefully to what is being asked, and formulate a logically ordered response to that question *only.* If you are asked to brief the case, start by saying, "The facts of this case are . . ." Then continue that way with the other items. Don't mingle the **facts** with the **procedural posture** or the **holding** with the **reasoning.** State one legal principle at a time, along with the language from which you drew it and then the implications that follow from it. Make linear arguments. One trick for written assignments: string the topic sentences together without the rest of the content of the paragraphs and see if they make logical sense.

Imagine you are asked—in class or on an exam—whether, under *Yates*, a person can be punished under §1519 for destroying a ledger that has on it blood evidence from a murder (law professors love to use bizarre hypotheticals!). One logical, linear answer might be along the following lines:

1. A ledger is both a record and a tangible object.
2. That suggests that it should be covered by §1519.
3. But the plurality interprets "tangible object" based on the meaning intended by Congress, and presumably would interpret "record" based on the meaning intended by Congress.
4. According to the plurality, Congress intended, in §1519, to punish only those who destroy "objects used to record or preserve information," and not as "an all-encompassing ban on the spoliation of evidence." (Notice the quotation of important language here.)
5. While a ledger is used to preserve information, it isn't usually used to preserve information about *blood.*
6. Therefore, I think the plurality would conclude that because Congress didn't intend to include this evidence in §1519, the person cannot be punished.

7. Justice Alito and the dissent, however, look only at the text of the statute.
8. A ledger is a "record."
9. Therefore, I think Justice Alito and the dissent would conclude that the person can be punished.

Note that although this is a good exam answer, in class you are not likely to be able to spit this answer out all at once! It will probably involve a lot of back-and-forth between you and the professor. But the closer you can hew to a logical order, the sharper and faster your dialogue with the professor will be. You will look and feel smart and successful.

Be Precise. Words like "it," "this," or "they," are imprecise. Substitute more precise language.

Imprecise	More Precise
It is a record.	*The ledger* is a record.
This means that Congress did not intend to cover a blood-soaked ledger.	*The argument that Congress intended to cover only records that preserve information* means that Congress did not intend to cover a blood-soaked ledger.
They said congressional intent is important.	*The plurality* said congressional intent is important.
He argued that he should win the case.	*The plaintiff* (or: *the defendant*) argued that he should win the case.

Just as it matters whether a statute uses "and" or "or," it matters whether you are talking about the plurality, the concurrence, or the dissent—and "they" does not convey that information.

Use legal terms, or the terms repeatedly used in the assigned reading, whenever possible. Talk about "tangible objects," not "things." If you have read a Rule that requires a lawyer to conduct "an inquiry reasonable under the circumstances" and the professor asks whether a lawyer has acted correctly, don't talk about whether the lawyer has "done the right thing" or "followed the rule" or "can be punished," but about whether the lawyer has conducted "an inquiry reasonable under the circumstances." *Then* you can draw a conclusion about rightness or punishment. These admonitions seem simple and obvious, but you would be surprised how many beginning law students ignore them. In their haste to answer a big question—"is this right or just?"—they skip over what is really being asked.

Be Concise. Answer the question being asked and *only* that question. Avoid irrelevant or redundant statements. Use simple, assertive statements rather than rambling run-on sentences. Answer the question, and then stop talking or writing.

All three rules—be organized, be precise, and be concise—also apply when you are volunteering in class, whether you are answering a question, asking a question, or participating in a discussion. To ensure that your contribution is relevant and not redundant, be sure to listen to your classmates. There is nothing more annoying to a professor (or classmates) than a student who asks a question that has just been asked and answered or makes a point that another student just made. If you don't understand an answer that's been given or a comment that's been made, you can ask about it—but don't simply ask the same question in different words.

Basically, successful legal communication all comes back to this: be prepared, and then listen and think before you speak.

* * *

As a beginning law student, you should try to use the skills and techniques that we talk about in this chapter from your first day of law school. But many techniques take a lot of practice, and that's a large part of what the first year of law school is all about. A good portion of "reading (and writing, thinking, and communicating) like a lawyer" is simply honing the skills and learning to apply them in the specific context of legal decision-making. The only way to do that is to practice those skills repeatedly, in many different legal contexts and on many different legal questions. You cannot learn or improve reading, reasoning, and communication skills by reading a book.

Chapter 3

THE STRUCTURE OF GOVERNMENT AND THE STRUCTURE OF LAW

Law school focuses on the study of law and the legal system. This obvious observation leads to an often overlooked one: a successful law student needs to understand the multiple and competing sources of law in America. Law professors generally assume that you have a firm grasp of the structure of government and are comfortable with ideas like divided government and public versus private law. But even undergraduate political science majors may find themselves struggling to translate what they knew before law school to the specific questions raised in law school. For example, when is the U.S. Supreme Court the final word on a law? Does the answer depend on whether the law is a statute or constitution or whether the source of the law is the federal or state government or a legislative or executive body? The answer, you may have guessed, depends on all of those things—and others too.

To be successful, you need to be able to answer the following questions: Where does the law come from? Who interprets the law and how? What happens if laws appear to conflict? Where does the legal system fit in the larger system of government? The answers to these questions require a confident understanding of the American system of government and the types of laws it produces. In this chapter we review the structure of government and the structure of law. Even though some of this material may be familiar, resist the urge to skim! You need to have these concepts clearly and solidly in mind as you prepare for class. The institutional design of government pervades everything we do in law school. So, be patient and careful as you read this chapter. If you already know some of these concepts, great—you can relax and enjoy the refresher. If they are new to you, you should return to this chapter again during the semester to reinforce your understanding. You should not worry if most—or almost all—are new or only vaguely familiar. Even lawyers find it helpful to review these concepts regularly.

THE STRUCTURE OF AMERICAN GOVERNMENT: A SYSTEM DIVIDED

The hallmark of American government is **division**. The country's founding document, the United States Constitution, divides the government **vertically** and **horizontally**. The government is divided vertically between the national (federal) government and the states. Each of the two vertical halves—the state and federal governments—are also divided horizontally into executive, legislative, and judicial branches.

Why did the Founding Generation, those who wrote and ratified the U.S. Constitution, divide power in so many complex ways? They were worried about abuse of governmental power and the possibility of majority tyranny. To protect citizens from the government and from each other, the Founding Generation avoided concentrating power into the hands of a few and instead divided it to protect liberty. States similarly sought to divide authority in their own governments.

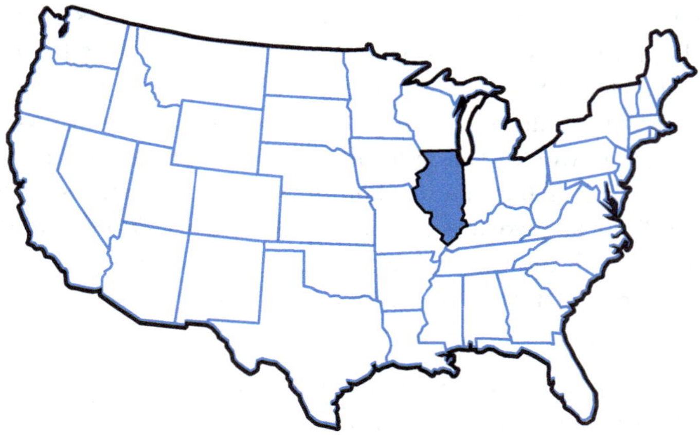

	EXECUTIVE	LEGISLATIVE	JUDICIAL
NATION	President	Congress	Federal Courts
STATE	Governor	State legislature	State courts

Vertical Division (Federalism) and Horizontal Division (Separation of Powers)

Vertical Division

The vertical division of power between the national government and the governments of the fifty states is known as **federalism.** Federalism recognizes **dual sovereignty** in state and federal governments. Each government is sovereign—the ultimate authority—in areas defined by the U.S. Constitution. The Constitution specifies the powers held by the national government and reserves for the states any powers which are not assigned or have not been exercised by the national government.

- The national government is one of **delegated and limited powers.** The federal government has only the authority given to it—explicitly or implicitly—by the U.S. Constitution. At most law schools, the initial course in Constitutional Law devotes substantial time to exploring the distribution of powers between the federal government and the states.

- The state governments have **residual power** (also known as plenary or reserved power). States can act unless their power is restricted by the U.S. Constitution, their own state constitutions, or a federal statute. The mere fact that the Constitution gives a power to the federal government does not necessarily mean that it has been taken away from the states: the state and federal governments often exercise *overlapping* authority. However, if the U.S. Congress passes a law within its authority, the federal statute **preempts** any conflicting state law within its scope.

The distinction between limited and residual powers is clear-cut in theory but fuzzy in application. Defining the boundaries of authority granted by the Constitution is a difficult and controversial task. Every U.S. Supreme Court term includes cases in which opponents debate whether a question can be answered by federal law or is instead left to the individual states. Even in those cases where parties agree that the federal government has the authority to act, they may disagree about whether the federal law is in conflict with (and therefore preempts) the state law in question. Finally, the fact that states and the federal government often have concurrent or overlapping authority makes the inquiry even more challenging. The point is, you have to understand the basic idea of federalism and its implications in order to learn the law. But you can expect law school to provide you with a greater understanding of the nuances of the doctrine.

Finally, you could imagine the vertical division of power as also including the individual. The Constitution imposes limits on both the state and federal governments' power over persons, protecting individual rights. These limits are contained in various parts of the Constitution, including the original Constitution, the Bill of Rights—the first ten amendments to the Constitution—and various other amendments (most importantly the Fourteenth Amendment). Almost all of these limits protect people against both the state and federal governments. They guarantee such rights and freedoms as freedom of religion, speech, press, assembly, and petition; the right to bear arms; the right of privacy; a fair trial; the "equal protection of the laws"; and protection against cruel and unusual punishments.

Horizontal Division

The government is divided horizontally into three branches: legislative, executive, and judicial. This division is known as **separation of powers**, or "**checks and balances**," because governmental power is divided to allow each branch to check the others and to balance competing interests and capacity. We focus on the separation of powers within the federal government, but the basic three-part structure is reflected in different forms in the states as well.

The constitutional structure of the federal government includes the following offices and bodies:

- The federal **legislative branch** is principally responsible for *enacting* the laws. The U.S. Congress is the federal legislature and is divided into two chambers, the Senate and the House of Representatives. Senators and representatives are elected by the voters in each state. One hundred senators and 435 representatives serve. Senators serve staggered six-year terms such that one-third are up for election every two years. Each state has two senators. Representatives (also called congressmen, congresswomen, or members of Congress) are elected for two-year terms, and membership is apportioned among the states according to population. Each state has to have at least one representative. Based on the 2020 census, California has the most with 52. Seven states have only one representative (but still have two senators each since the Senate is not apportioned based on population).
- The federal **executive branch** is principally responsible for *enforcing* the laws. The president is the head of the executive branch. (The state executive is a governor, as reflected in the map graphic.) The president is elected for a four-year term by the members of the Electoral College, who are themselves elected by the voters in each state. The Twenty-second Amendment limits a president to two terms.
- The federal **judicial branch** is principally responsible for *interpreting* laws. The judicial branch consists of the U.S. Supreme Court and lower federal courts (as we explore in great detail in Chapter 4). Federal judges are nominated by the president and confirmed by the Senate.

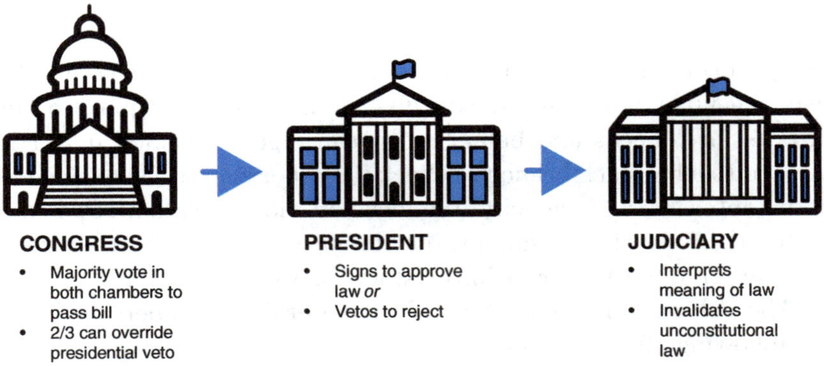

The Federal Lawmaking Process

All three branches play a role in the process of making federal law. First, for any federal statute to be enacted, a majority in both the House and the Senate must vote in favor of it. The House and Senate rely on committees and subcommittees to do their work. They follow different formal rules and informal practices in considering possible legislation. The history of the enactment of a bill, including committee reports, debates, and votes, is called **legislative history** and may be relevant to the law's eventual interpretation.

Every bill passed by the House and Senate is next presented to the president. The president has only two choices: sign it or veto it. If the president signs the bill, it becomes law. If the president vetoes the bill, it returns to the Congress. If two-thirds of the House and two-thirds of the Senate both vote to approve the bill again, they override the president's veto and the bill becomes law. If Congress fails to override the president's veto, it does not become law. The president must consider the bill as a whole: there is no power to veto certain portions of a law and accept other portions of law. Many states instead grant their governors a right to amend a law before signing it.

Courts do not formally participate in the process by which a bill becomes a law, but they do affect those laws. Judges will decide disputes over the meaning and application of the statute. In order to resolve those cases, judges interpret the law and explain its scope and implications. More significantly, courts may find that a duly enacted statute (federal or state) is inconsistent with the Constitution and invalidate the law because the Constitution overrides any inconsistent laws.

Any branch can decide that a law is unconstitutional, but all must agree that it *is* constitutional for a law to stand. If Congress believes a proposed law is unconstitutional, Congress will not enact it; if the president believes it is unconstitutional, the president will veto it; and if a court believes it is unconstitutional, the court will strike it down. While Congress and the president can oppose a law for any reason, a court can only vote against a law (invalidate it) if it is unconstitutional.

The Constitution creates three branches of government, but today a "fourth branch" is nearly as important: **administrative agencies.** Many aspects of our lives are affected by the work of agencies: health (Center for Disease Control or CDC), airline safety (National Transportation Safety Board or NTSB), housing (Department of Housing and Urban Development or HUD), employment (Department of Labor), capital markets (Securities and Exchange Commission or SEC), and communication (Federal Communication Commission or FCC). Indeed, it is hard to think of an area untouched by administrative agencies.

Congress (or the president) may create administrative agencies and assign certain responsibilities to them. Many agencies operate within the executive branch, including 15 cabinet-level departments such as Defense or Education and executive agencies like the Central Intelligence Agency. In addition, there are more than 50 independent agencies such as the Federal Reserve Board and the Securities and Exchange Commission. The president typically appoints agency leadership with Senate consent. But the great majority of agency employees are civil service workers, hired like any other governmental employee. Agencies wield significant authority to determine how individuals, companies, and even cities and states must act. They often have a mix of legislative, executive, and judicial power. Not surprisingly given their many forms and processes, the rules governing agencies are complex and changing.

THE STRUCTURE OF AMERICAN LAW: A NETWORKED SYSTEM

Having reviewed the structure of American government, we now focus on law itself. The hallmark of American law is diversity. Laws come in many types and are produced by many sources. And because of the natural imprecision and ambiguity of language, laws may be susceptible to many meanings, some of which might depend on the context, application, and decision-maker. It will help you to navigate the network of laws if you understand two essential aspects of it:

- Laws are divided into both vertical and horizontal hierarchies that correspond to the sources and types of law.
- The question of how laws are interpreted, and by whom, pervades our legal system.

Sources and Types of Law: Vertical and Horizontal Hierarchies

We talk about "law" as though it is a single thing. But law comes from many sources and in many types, which affect how we read and understand a law. Even more important, source and type determine the relative authority and effect of a law. They tell us, in other words, both to whom the law applies and what happens when two laws conflict.

Sources of law are vertically hierarchical: laws from higher sources supersede laws from lower sources. But each source produces various **types of laws**, and among laws from the same source, some types of laws are superior to others. We might call that superiority a matter of horizontal hierarchy.

What Are the Sources of American Law? By and large, they are the different governments within our American system: the federal government, state governments, and local governments. These three governments form a vertical hierarchy, with the local governments at the bottom and the federal government on top. Each of these sources produces multiple types of law, and most of the time, laws from a higher source supersede every type of law from a lower source.

The source of the legislation determines not only its place in the hierarchy but also its scope. The law can only reach people who are within that government's authority. For example, local law governs only residents of (or visitors to) that city. The state laws of New York can't reach to California but can cover every city within New York State. Federal law applies to the whole country. People are subject to laws from many sources. If you are in Nashville, you are subject to the laws of metropolitan Nashville (local), Tennessee (state), and the United States (federal).

What Are the Types of Law? Constitutions, legislation, rules and administrative regulations, and common law make up most of American law. And they are in that pecking order, with constitutions on top and common law on the bottom.

The two hierarchies, of sources and of types, give us a simple map of the complex system of American law. Federal law is superior to state law which is superior to local law. And *within* each of those three levels of government, the constitution is superior to legislation which is superior to regulation which is superior to common law.

Now let's turn to the details of the types of law—in their horizontal hierarchical order—keeping in mind that not every source produces every type of law.

Constitutions (and charters) are foundational documents. The first task for any new country—after a revolution, a declaration of independence, or other founding event—is to draft a constitution. Constitutions establish the framework for government; they specify how the new government is to be organized and selected and how laws other than the constitution may be enacted. Most constitutional provisions are directed only at parts of government; unlike ordinary laws, they don't usually tell private citizens how to behave. Also, unlike other laws, constitutions are usually created—and amended—by extraordinary means: special conventions, supermajorities, or direct voter referenda. The U.S. Constitution, for example, was drafted by a special national convention in 1787 and then ratified by individual conventions in the 13 states over the next two years. Amendments to the federal Constitution likewise require an extraordinary level of consensus: approval by two-thirds of each house of Congress and ratification by three-quarters of the states. Amendments have been successfully ratified only 27 times (and the first ten amendments were ratified all at once). Every state has its own unique constitution. Local governments often have foundational laws as well, although these are usually labeled charters rather than constitutions.

Because constitutions are foundational, difficult to amend, and designed to endure over long periods of time, they are usually written in very general language. Combine vague language with crucial subject matter and the result is contentious debates over the meaning of the law. You can expect to devote a great deal of time to constitutional interpretation in courses devoted to the Constitution, such as Constitutional Law and Criminal Procedure. Some other courses, including Civil Procedure and Family Law, will focus on constitutional interpretation for some topics.

The next level of sources is **legislation.** Individual pieces of legislation might variously be referred to as statutes, acts, ordinances, or codes. Laws passed by the federal and state governments are more likely to be called statutes or acts; laws adopted by county or city councils are more likely to be called ordinances or codes.

Legislation is enacted by ordinary legislative means, by a state or federal legislature or a city council (sometimes with the participation of the executive branch) and can be changed the same way. In the federal system, as we noted, statutes must be passed by both houses of Congress and signed by the president (unless Congress overrides a presidential veto). Legislation can be directed to governmental officials or to private citizens. These types of laws are often long and detailed, presenting their own interpretive challenges.

Legislative enactments will govern within their geographic sphere unless they are inconsistent with a source of authority that is superior on either the vertical or horizontal axis. Thus, state legislation that conflicts with federal legislation is invalid because federal legislation is vertically superior, and state legislation that conflicts with the state constitution is invalid because the state constitution is horizontally superior.

The interactions get more complicated as we consider **rules** and **administrative regulations.** Administrative regulations are promulgated by administrative agencies, under authority delegated to them by a congressionally enacted statute. For example, Congress has delegated the implementation of the Clean Air Act to the Environmental Protection Agency (EPA). Pursuant to that statutory authority, the EPA enacts regulations that specify precisely what quantities of specific pollutants may be emitted by any given source.

Each statute is different, and so the scope of different agencies' authority will vary. Because agencies may have greater or lesser scopes of authority, one question about any agency regulation is always whether it is within the power of the agency to create. This requires statutory interpretation of a particular kind. We have to ask whether the statute actually delegates to the agency (1) the general authority to promulgate the particular regulation, and (2) the ability to do so by the procedures that the agency used for promulgating the particular regulation. For example, for the EPA to regulate greenhouse gases as "pollutants" under the Clean Air Act, greenhouse gases must meet the statutory definition of "pollutants" and the regulation must be issued using a procedure called "notice-and-comment rulemaking" (because that's what the Clean Air Act requires—you need not worry about exactly what it means).

In law school, you will focus primarily on federal agencies. But in law practice and to a limited extent in school, you will also deal with state and local agencies that derive their authority from state and local elected bodies. Administrative Law and similar courses focus on the fascinating and complex relationship between administrative agencies and the elected bodies that govern them.

Rules are adopted by governments to manage their internal processes. Some of the most important rules that you will learn in law school dictate how courts function. The Rules Enabling Act (a federal statute) delegates to the Supreme Court "the power to prescribe general rules of practice and procedure and rules of evidence" for federal courts. These rules can be amended by the Supreme Court, but they can also be changed, or even vetoed, by ordinary congressional legislation. The Supreme Court, with the help of specially appointed committees of experts, has enacted Rules of Civil Procedure, Rules of Appellate Procedure, Rules of Criminal Procedure, and Rules of Evidence, among others. In most contexts, the various rules are treated like statutes, but there are some differences. In most law schools, eponymous classes like Civil Procedure and Evidence cover one body of rules as well as related laws.

Common law is made by judges to fill in the gaps in statutory or other authority. We'll talk more about the common law—which has multiple meanings—in Chapter 4. For now, you need to know that it is at the bottom of the hierarchy: anything the legislature or any other authority enacts can overrule the common law.

In addition, there are two other types of "law" that do not fit neatly into the hierarchies:

International law is established by agreements, such as treaties, between two or more countries. In the U.S., only the federal government can enter into such accords. Treaties may grant rights only to countries or may create rights in individuals. Treaties, like statutes, must be consistent with the federal Constitution. If a treaty conflicts with a statute, the more recent one usually controls. As the world's problems have become increasingly transnational, international law-making has become correspondingly more important.

Model laws and Restatements of Law are *not* law. Both *influence* the law. They are created by groups of legal experts. Model laws are blueprints for statutes and include the Uniform Commercial Code (studied in Contracts) and the Model Penal Code (Criminal Law). Restatements present a single, consistent statement of the law in a specific area. They may reflect a majority position or the recommended one. Restatements become law if adopted by judges or legislatures.

CONSTITUTION *(CHARTER)*	CREATES government. General and hard-to-amend.
LEGISLATION *(STATUTES, ACTS, CODES)*	Enacted by ELECTED OFFICIALS. More concrete. Easier to revise and amend.
REGULATIONS	Create REQUIREMENTS for acts. Highly detailed. Produced (and changed) by agencies.
RULES	Set Operating PROCEDURES for government. Very specific. Eastiest to change.
COMMON LAW	Produced by COURTS. General principles developed and applied in specific disputes over time. Can be overruled by courts or by legislatures.

Types of Laws

We've just done a lot of heavy lifting, so let's review. The *source* of the law is the level of government from which it derives: federal, state, or local. The *type* of law is the form that it takes: constitutions, legislation, rules and administrative regulations, or common law. Conflicts between any two laws are resolved first in favor of the hierarchically superior source, and within the laws from each source, in favor of the hierarchically superior type.

Of course, there are caveats and exceptions to this basic explanation of how to resolve conflicts. Federal common law, for example, trumps state sources of authority only in very limited contexts (a complicated subject known as the *Erie* doctrine, which will probably be covered in your Civil Procedure class). International law plays a role, as do model statutes and Restatements of Law. Local governments are organized differently across (and even within) the states.

Don't be too concerned about these specific deviations: you can learn them as you need them. For now, you just need an overview of the general pattern, a roadmap of American law.

And just like an ordinary roadmap, the legal roadmap has a system of directions to guide us to different places. You will see these directions in the very first assignment you read for your first class. The opinion will include references to a decision by a specific court, legislation adopted by a state or the federal government, or rules of procedure controlling the court's actions or even all three. Do not be intimidated by these short directions! They are as simple as learning that "Ave." refers to the road (avenue) that you should take and "N." means to head north. They are just unfamiliar to you now, but you will learn more about these abbreviations and number combinations in Chapter 4 and in your Legal Research class. You will soon forget when these directions were new—just as you do not think about the fact that when directions say "Exit 79" it means you should take the highway exit marked "79."

Interpretation

Law always requires interpretation because the meaning of a law is not self-evident. How a statute, a regulation, a common law doctrine, or any other type of law applies to the particular facts at hand depends on what the law actually means—this might be more or less clear, and someone will have to interpret it. Sometimes interpreting a law will be easy, but more often—especially in the cases you read in your first-year courses—it will be hard. We will break down the question of interpretation into questions of who interprets and how they interpret.

Test Your Understanding

To appreciate the inherent ambiguity in law, it is helpful to start with a simple legal rule: "No vehicles are allowed in the park." This seems straightforward. But consider the following questions. And begin the process of thinking like a lawyer by making the best possible arguments for each side!

1. Does the ordinance prohibit bicycles from being used in the park? Skateboards? Electric scooters? Wheelchairs? Hot air balloons? Horses? Horse-drawn carriages?
2. Suppose a society of World War II veterans wants to put a memorial in the park. Does the ordinance prohibit a statue of a tank? A real tank rendered permanently nonfunctional? A tank that is nonfunctional, but could function again if repaired? A tank that is fully restored and in good repair, but is bolted down? A fully functional tank?

Who Interprets Law? Most 1L classes focus on interpretations by courts. But judges are not the only people who interpret law. An agency official determining whether someone has met the requirements of a regulation, such as a health inspector evaluating the cleanliness of a kitchen, is interpreting the regulation as the rule applies to the circumstances. Likewise, a lawyer interprets the law when advising clients, perhaps about whether a contract would be enforceable if the client's needs changed. A court is asked to interpret a law only when some dispute arises such as the restaurant owner challenging a poor health code rating or two contract parties disagreeing about their responsibilities.

Judges effectively have the final responsibility for interpreting *all* laws. Judges interpret laws produced by federal, state, and local governments. Judges interpret laws produced by founders, legislators, executives, agencies, and other judges. But judges may defer to the interpretations of others in certain circumstances. For example:

- Congress enacts a statute. Somebody sues, alleging that the federal Constitution (a higher authority, remember) denies Congress the authority to pass the statute. Maybe it violates someone's constitutional rights, or maybe it is outside of Congress's constitutionally granted powers. A court has to decide whether the statute is constitutional. In short, a judge has to interpret both the challenged statute and the Constitution in order to determine whether the law is consistent or inconsistent with the Constitution. How much deference should the judge give to Congress's implicit determination that it *did* have the constitutional authority to pass the statute, that is, to Congress's own interpretation of the Constitution?
- Congress enacts a statute delegating to an administrative agency the authority to promulgate regulations implementing the statute. The agency does so. Somebody sues, alleging that the regulation is not within the agency's statutorily granted authority. Again, a court will have to interpret the federal statute in order to determine whether it grants the agency the power to promulgate the particular regulation. But the agency has already interpreted the statute as *granting* the agency that power. How much deference should the court give to the agency's interpretation?

The two most important factors to consider in answering these questions are **institutional competence** and **democratic accountability**—factors that can sometimes be in tension with each other. Both factors are related to separation of powers concerns and the reasons that the Constitution allocates certain authority to certain branches.

- Institutional competence reflects how well-suited a body is to a certain task. Analyzing institutional competence for legal interpretation entails making a judgment about whether a court, legislature, or executive is better at interpreting the Constitution, a statute, or other law. The answer is not clear!

It depends on the institution's resources, structure, incentives, experience, and expertise.

- Democratic accountability means that officials are responsive to the public. It ensures that citizens can monitor, and if necessary, overrule, governmental decisions with which they disagree. Congress and the president are accountable through elections. Federal judges are not, but most state judges are. Although you might think that democratic accountability should always prevail, sometimes we *want* interpretation by a democratically unaccountable institution—for example in deciding whether a statute enacted by the majority violates individual constitutional rights.

The relative importance of competence and accountability depend on the law and the application of that law. Institutional competence takes on much more significance in some situations. Imagine that the agency has unquestioned power to promulgate *some* regulation on the topic (for example, specifying the amount of pollutants that may be discharged by a particular industry per year, undeniably within the purview of the EPA), and the question is whether regulation of a particular substance (greenhouse gases) is authorized by the statute. At that point, the agency's scientific expertise is likely to trump the other factors and suggest deference.

How Do Judges Interpret Laws? It depends on the type of law being interpreted. Let's begin by considering statutory interpretation. Statutes are often unclear despite the legislature's best intentions (or because of them!). Statutes can be ambiguous for any number of reasons, including the collective process of their creation, the intricacies of their application, and the mutability of the English language.

The basic task is to figure out what the legislature meant. Courts use these interpretive tools, many of which we saw in the *Yates* case in Chapter 2:

- Text. What does the statute say? Courts always start here. In all but the easiest cases, text won't resolve the particular question.
- Context. How does the specific rule fit into the overall statute (or set of statutes)? A court might look at other parts of the

statute for clues about the purpose of the statute or about how the particular provision is supposed to work.

- Legislative history. What did the enacting body say? The history of the statute's enactment, including committee reports, legislative debates, and so on, might also help courts divine the meaning of the statute.
- Goals. Why was it enacted? The legislature was trying to accomplish *something* and knowing what problems it was trying to solve might help us figure out what the statute means.
- Precedent. What have courts said? Prior cases interpreting various parts of the statute can also provide guidance. They ensure that courts treat the statute as a coherent whole. In addition, courts look at prior judicial interpretations of similar language from other statutes. Especially if those earlier cases were decided before the legislature enacted the statute at issue, we might think that the legislature intended to use the same language in the same way.
- Canons of construction. How do we generally interpret statutes? These are standard guidelines to help courts parse difficult statutes. One common example is "*expressio unius est exclusio alterius,*" meaning the expression of the one is the exclusion of the other. Application of this canon suggests that if the statute contains a list (such as permitted or prohibited actions, or of items or actions that should be treated a particular way), the legislature intended that statutory language to apply *only* to items on the list. Unfortunately, canons often point in opposite directions. Another canon is that "like should be treated alike," which will often conflict with "*expressio unius*."
- Constitutionality. How do we make the statute valid? There is a presumption in favor of interpreting statutes so that they do not conflict with the Constitution. Thus, if one plausible interpretation makes the statute constitutional and another makes it unconstitutional, the courts will adopt the former. This presumption also applies in the context of treaties: a statute will not be interpreted to alter a treaty obligation unless Congress makes clear its intent to do so.

In the end, all these techniques might still leave us with only a general purpose and an ambiguous text. Different theories of statutory interpretation use these techniques in distinct ways, and scholars and judges often debate which method is appropriate and which techniques are best or most important. Ultimately, though, statutory interpretation requires judgment. Courts must interpret imprecise language in a way that they believe best captures the legislative meaning, although "meaning" is itself ambiguous as it might mean what the legislature *said* or what it *meant* or *tried to say*—see how difficult statutory interpretation can be?

Statutes are only one of the sources of law that present difficult questions of interpretation. In some ways, statutory interpretation is the easiest type of interpretation because the goal is clear: do what the legislature tells you to do. Interpretation of federal rules (of Evidence, Civil Procedure, and so on) are similar, although each presents unique challenges. Interpreting agency regulations is messier, as it requires courts to integrate the regulation with other regulations *and* with the underlying statute. Even interpreting judicial precedent in order to figure out the common law is harder than it looks—as you will learn as you go through your first year of law school!

Constitutional interpretation is the most controversial because people cannot even agree on the interpretive goal: is it to implement the original meaning of the Constitution as understood by its authors? Or is it to implement a modern understanding of the Constitution? If discovering the purpose of a statute passed last year is difficult, imagine the problems in trying to find—and apply to contemporary issues—the purposes of a constitution written over the course of the last several centuries. And if the proper goal is to implement modern understandings, whose understandings count? These questions are much too big to explore in this introductory material, but you will find them discussed often in any course that includes constitutional topics.

The primary lesson here is not that interpretation is difficult—although it is. Nor is it that you have to tailor the interpretive method to the particular document you're interpreting—although you do. The main lesson is that ambiguity, uncertainty, and interpretive discretion are unavoidable. But that's part of what makes law and the work of a lawyer (and law student) challenging and interesting!

Recognize and embrace ambiguity, but be careful. Just because clearly right answers in law are few and far between doesn't mean that there are no clearly wrong answers. For example, there may be several different plausible interpretations of a statute or a precedent, but some interpretations are not reasonable. Take our "no vehicles in the park" ordinance: it's simply implausible to argue that it prohibits people from walking their dogs in the park, even if we're not sure whether it prohibits a dog pulling a child's sled. Over the course of your first year you will learn the art of distinguishing reasonable legal arguments from unreasonable ones, and plausible interpretations from implausible ones. Where to place the line is often unclear and even controversial, but there is a line.

Test Your Understanding

Return to the question whether the "no vehicles in the park" statute applies to bicycles. Here is some further information to help you interpret the statute:

1. The city council enacted it after a child was hit by a car in the park. At the city council meeting, some council members focused on safety concerns. Others stated that the park should be a quiet place for rest and relaxation. Still others were worried about the environment, noting that if they could, they would prohibit vehicles anywhere inside the city limits.
2. A court had previously interpreted a statute requiring that "all vehicles stop and pull to the side of the road" whenever an emergency vehicle approaches with its siren going. The court held that that statute included bicycles.

The study of American law is interesting, challenging, and complex because American law is all of those things. This chapter provides you with an understanding of lawmaking that will help you in many of your 1L courses. Similar interpretive questions arise whether you are interpreting a statute or rule in Civil Procedure, a constitutional provision in Constitutional Law, or a contract in Contracts.

But *law* consists of much more than *laws*. The next chapter focuses on legal *institutions*—those entities and people who put the law into action.

Chapter 4

THE STRUCTURE OF THE AMERICAN LEGAL SYSTEM

The American legal system consists of a network of governmental bodies that resolve disputes. You are already familiar with the most important part of the structure: courts. American popular culture, from novels to TV shows and the news media, reveals different pieces of the court system. As a law student, you can take advantage of this existing knowledge as you work to learn it in a more thorough and complete way. This chapter is designed to give you two perspectives on the system: the full landscape and specific features. We'll start at 30,000 feet with the distinctive features of the U.S. legal system so you can get a general sense of the system that has developed to handle disputes. We'll then descend and get in closer to help you to learn (and memorize) names and functions of key parts.

LEGAL SYSTEMS

Creating a legal system involves choices. The American system is adversarial rather than inquisitorial. It is based on common law rather than civil law. It includes both public law and private law. Each choice has far-reaching effects on the courts and law.

Adversarial versus Inquisitorial

Most of the world has adopted an **inquisitorial** legal regime. In an inquisitorial system, there is generally no jury. The judge is in charge of all aspects of the case: the judge investigates the facts, researches the law, structures the lawsuit, and decides the outcome. The lawyers contribute arguments and suggestions, but the judge is an active participant, not simply a neutral referee.

The United States takes a different approach. American courts are **adversarial.** Legal questions are resolved through a competition between the two sides to dispute. In criminal cases, a state or federal **prosecutor** brings a charge (usually through an "indictment") against a criminal **defendant**, accusing the defendant of violating the law. A civil case (or "civil action") begins with a lawsuit filed by a **plaintiff** against a **defendant.** Both sides argue vigorously and fully on their own behalf. It's a system that is trial-focused and lawyer-driven, with the judge (and the jury) serving only as neutral referees.

No system is purely adversarial or purely inquisitorial. Even in the American system, the judge can sometimes play an active role. Nevertheless, the American legal system is widely recognized as the most adversarial in the world. It is also distinctive among adversarial systems in the degree of its reliance on juries: American courts use juries more frequently than even the British, who invented the jury. Thus, two defining features of the American legal system are that (1) it is adversarial rather than inquisitorial, and (2) it allows juries to play a large role.

Common Law and Civil Law

America has a common law system rather than a civil law system. In **civil law** (or **civilian**) countries, the law is determined entirely by a written code. Judges decide cases based on the code, but those decisions technically have no influence on the resolution of future cases;

only the code itself is binding. In **common law** countries, by contrast, the judges make binding law as they decide cases. (This fact helps explain why you might read some old English cases: because our common law is derived from English common law, tracing a judicial doctrine back to its source might require reading an English opinion.) In common law countries, judicial opinions serve as **precedent** in two different ways. If there is no statute or other enacted law to consult, prior opinions are the only source of law. Many areas of American law are dominated by judge-made law, including the law governing personal injuries (torts) and promises (contract law). But even if the case is governed by a statute, regulation, or constitution, prior judicial interpretations of that law govern the law's interpretation in later cases.

To see how important the common law versus civil law distinction is, let's use a simple fact pattern: a bicyclist receives a traffic ticket for riding in the park. The cyclist then goes to court to challenge the ticket, arguing that bicycles are permitted in the park.

- Imagine the bicyclist lives in a common law country. What sources will the court consult to resolve the complaint? If the city has adopted an ordinance stating "No vehicles in the park," the court will consider the statute itself as well as any earlier judicial decisions applying the statute in the same or similar circumstances (remember the *Test Your Understanding* example in Chapter 3). If there is no city ordinance, the common law court will look at prior court cases involving vehicles in the park, park safety, or bicycle use.
- Imagine the bicyclist lives in a civil law country. If the city has adopted the "no vehicles in the park" ordinance, the civil law court will look only at the statute itself and will not consider any prior court rulings on the statute. If there is no city ordinance, the civil law court still considers only statutes. Without a statute specifically on bikes in the park, the court will resort to statutes on a more general topic like the city's power to issue citations.

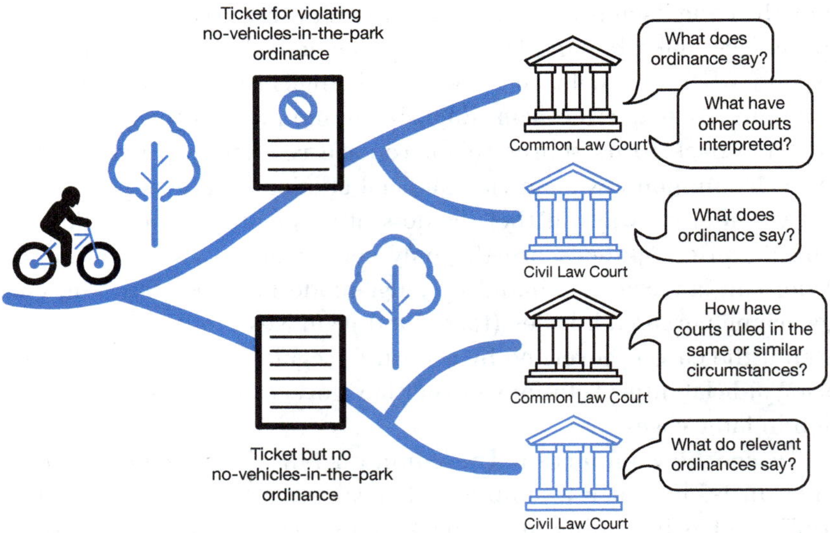

Vehicles in the Park

Judges make decisions in very different ways in common law and civil law countries, and their written rulings reflect those different approaches. Civil law judges discuss and cite only the language of codes and constitutions. They do not mention other cases. American judges, like other common law judges, rely primarily on other cases, trying to determine how a case should be decided in a way that remains faithful to those precedents. As we showed you in Chapter 2, part of what you will learn in your first year is how to draw analogies between cases—that is, how to argue that a particular problem is or is not governed by a prior case. Common law reasoning is a central part of an American lawyer's work.

We have been distinguishing between the concepts of common law and civil law based on the regime or legal system that each describes. But "common law" and "civil law" are also used to mean other related but separate concepts. Just as a common law legal system is defined by judges making law, the term common law can refer to judicial opinions being the source of law on a question. Thus, when we say that the fundamental principles of contract law are principally common law, we mean that they are based on cases rather than statutes. Likewise, civil law means that the source of law is a written code of some sort.

While we cannot list all the ways in which the terms may be used, we can note the most frequent ones that you'll see in law school. Common law can be contrasted to equity: a common law court hears disputes requesting monetary relief (damages) while an equity (or chancery) court resolves cases seeking equitable relief (an order such as an injunction). Civil can be contrasted to criminal: a civil action is a private legal action, which can be filed by a person, company, or the government. A criminal action can only be brought by the government. Another way to look at it is that civil lawsuits redress wrongs committed by the defendant against a person or institution (including the government itself) and a criminal prosecution redresses wrongs done to *both* the private party *and* society as a whole.

Private Law and Public Law

The American legal system includes both public law and private law. In general, **public law** governs the relationships between the *government* and individuals (or corporations or other entities), and **private law** governs the relationships among *private* actors such as people or businesses. The first year of law school usually includes some public law courses such as Criminal Law or Constitutional Law. Upper-class courses in public law include regulatory courses such as Tax and Environmental Law. The first year also includes private law courses: Torts, Contracts, and Property. Corporations is an example of a common upper-class course that focuses primarily on private law.

For public law, the government sets all the rules: individuals are not permitted to agree among themselves, for example, that their behavior is not criminal or that a particular business transaction will be exempt from taxation. But in private law areas, while the framework and default rules are sometimes established by legislatures or courts, individuals (and corporations) have a lot of leeway to structure their agreements in ways that change, avoid, or simply fill in the large gaps in those rules. In other words, people can enter into agreements that, practically speaking, have the effect of law.

Public law and private law often intersect, creating a complex web of relationships. For example, the relationship between an employer and its employees is governed partly by public law and partly by private law. State and federal laws prohibit the employer from discriminating in various ways, require it to negotiate with labor unions, and establish minimum wages and maximum hours. But the employer and employee are mostly free to bargain and set their own rules about salary, promotions, working conditions, cause for termination, and the like. If an employer discriminates, either the government or the employee can take the employer to court for violation of state and federal antidiscrimination laws: that's public law. If the employer fails to pay the employee the agreed-upon salary, however, the employee can sue for breach of contract: that's private law.

With the expansion of state and federal regulation, private parties' interactions with public law are increasingly pervasive. Huge sections of American industry are subject to both general regulations (such as environmental regulations) and industry-specific regulations (such as emissions standards for new automobiles). Much of this regulatory activity takes place in administrative agencies rather than in courts and legislatures. Nevertheless, because many of your first-year courses will focus on judicial decisions—and agency procedures are a specialized topic—we focus on the court system in the next few sections of this chapter.

COURTS

The United States is divided between a single national government and multiple state governments (this vertical division, or **federalism**, is described in detail in Chapter 3). Each government has created its own set of courts. We will focus on the federal court system because it is important and offers a structure that is reflected in various forms in the states. Each state court system is unique, but you will not be expected to know all of those differences. However, we will note significant distinctions when they are important. In 1L, you will be reading cases from many different jurisdictions.

Just as the U.S. Constitution establishes the parameters of federal authority and the work of the elected branches, it also sets forth five significant aspects of the federal judiciary:

1. The judicial branch is headed by a Supreme Court.
2. Congress has the power to create lower federal courts.

3. The president nominates and the Senate confirms judges who serve on the Supreme Court and lower federal courts.
4. Judges have life tenure and can only be removed through an impeachment process.
5. The jurisdiction of the federal courts is set by Congress within boundaries set by the Constitution.

Article III of the Constitution sets forth these requirements, and hence we call these courts **Article III courts.** But the Constitution leaves out a lot of important details. So, everything else of significance —from the size of the Supreme Court to the organization of the lower courts to the actual jurisdiction of each federal court—is prescribed by federal statute. Similarly, each state determines the shape of its own judicial branch by some combination of constitutional and statutory provisions.

The Dual Court Systems in the United States

Each system, state or federal, is organized into a hierarchy of courts. Cases ordinarily begin at the first tier and can work their way up to the highest tier. The state and federal systems exist side by side, and litigants often have a choice of which system to use.

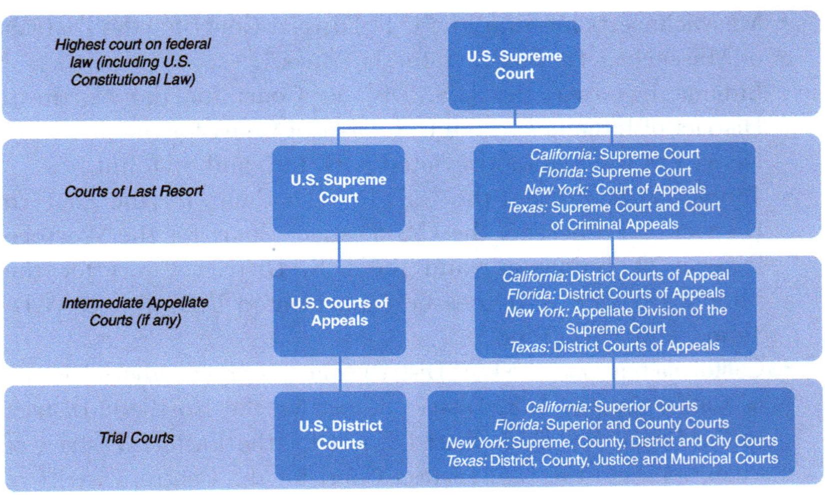

Dual Court System

What follows is a simplified description of how the state and federal courts are organized. You should be aware that there are variations and exceptions for almost everything we discuss. Nevertheless, the basic outlines of this generic system are enough for all but the most specialized legal areas.

The lowest courts in the hierarchy are the trial courts, where cases begin. In the federal system, they are called **United States District Courts**. In state systems, trial courts have a variety of names; most commonly they are called superior courts, but they may also be called circuit courts, county courts, or district courts among many other names. (States and their subdivisions, such as counties and municipalities, often also have specialized courts with limited jurisdiction, such as family courts, small claims courts, traffic courts, probate courts, juvenile courts, and municipal courts.) Trial courts are the only courts in which trials occur, and they are also the only courts that use juries. Each case gets a single trial judge; the trial judge may decide the case alone or with a jury, but almost never with other judges.

Each U.S. district court has multiple district judges. The districts are geographically defined, with each state containing between one and four district courts. The number of districts depends on population and caseload. For example:

- Massachusetts has *one*, the U.S. District Court for the District of Massachusetts (abbreviated D. Mass.).
- Indiana has *two*, the U.S. District Court for the Northern District of Indiana and the U.S. District Court for the Southern District of Indiana (abbreviated N.D. Ind. and S.D. Ind.).
- Tennessee has *three*, the U.S. District Court for the Eastern District of Tennessee, the U.S. District Court for the Western District of Tennessee, and the U.S. District Court for the Middle District of Tennessee (abbreviated E.D. Tenn., W.D. Tenn., and M.D. Tenn.).
- California has *four*, the U.S. District Court for the Southern District of California, the U.S. District Court for the Northern District of California, the U.S. District Court for the Eastern District of California, and the U.S. District Court for the Central District of California (abbreviated S.D. Cal., N.D. Cal., E.D. Cal., and C.D. Cal.). See the map on page 89.

Map of the U.S. District Courts in California

Apart from the District of Wyoming (which includes a small piece of Montana and Idaho), all federal district courts are entirely within a single state and do not cross state borders. You can learn more about federal courts by going to the Administrative Office of the U.S. Courts website: http://www.uscourts.gov.

If a party involved in a lawsuit does not like the result in a trial court, the party can appeal the decision to a court of review, often called an "appellate" court. The party challenging the trial court outcome is the **appellant**. The appellant will request that the appellate court **reverse** (overturn) or **vacate** (void) all or part of the trial court's decision. The responding party, known as the **appellee**, asks the trial court to **affirm** the lower court. In the federal system and many (but not all) states, there are two levels of appellate courts: an intermediate court of appeals and a final court of appeals. The federal intermediate courts are called **United States Courts of Appeals** (see the map on page 90). The country is divided into twelve geographic regions known as "circuits," and each circuit has its own court of appeals. These twelve circuits cover one or more district courts and one or more contiguous states and/or territories. Eleven of these courts are identified by number. The twelfth covers only the District of Columbia and is known as the U.S. Court of Appeals for the District of Columbia (D.C.) Circuit. The only court of appeals whose jurisdiction is defined by subject matter rather than by geography is the U.S. Court of Appeals for the Federal Circuit (also located

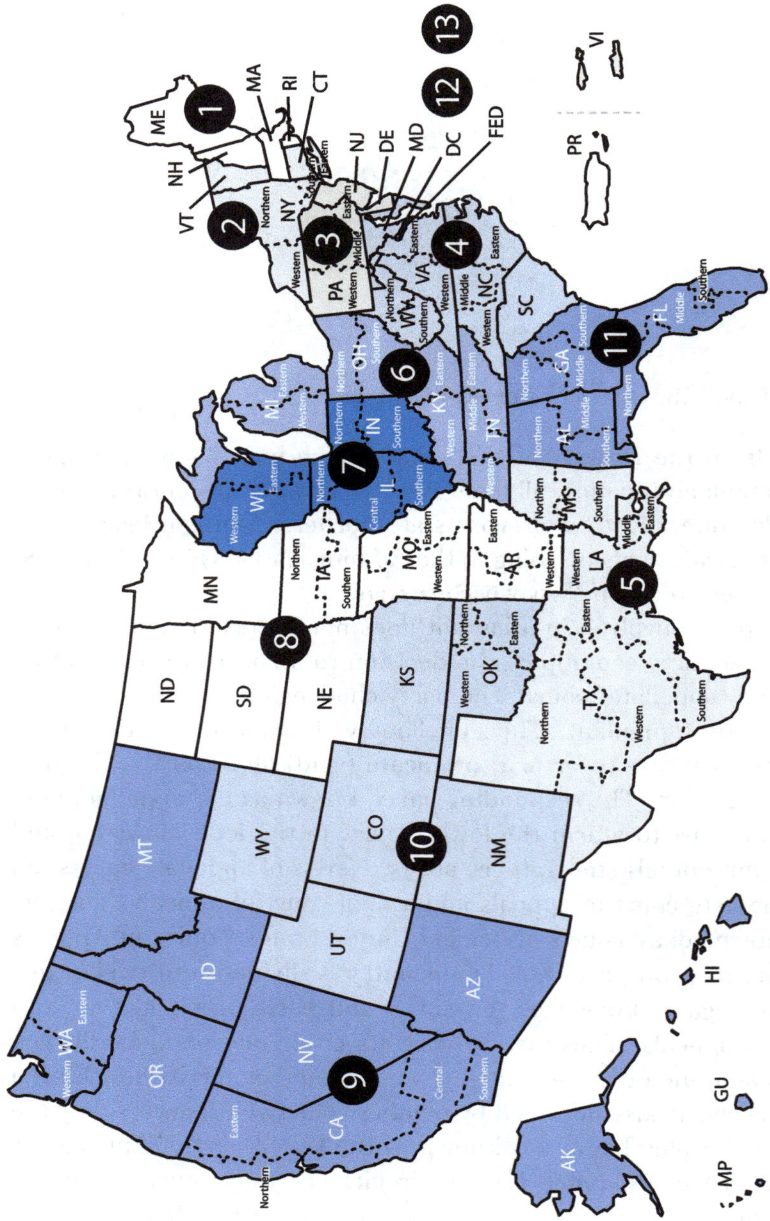

Map of the U.S. Courts of Appeals

in Washington, D.C.): it has jurisdiction over certain types of cases, including most patent cases, many tax cases, and many cases involving contracts with the federal government.

Test Your Understanding

> You have just lost a case in the Southern District of Florida. In which U.S. court of appeals must you file your appeal? Please see the map on page 90.

The jurisdiction of the federal courts of appeals (and of most intermediate state appellate courts) is mandatory rather than discretionary. If a court's jurisdiction is mandatory, it *must* hear cases that fall within its jurisdiction. If a court's jurisdiction is discretionary, it may choose which cases to hear and decide. As we will see, the U.S. Supreme Court (and some state supreme courts) exercises discretionary review in most circumstances.

U.S. courts of appeals may have anywhere from 6 to 29 circuit judges, but they decide most cases in groups ("panels") of three judges. Circuit panels may comprise active circuit judges, retired ("senior") circuit judges, district judges selected ("designated") by the chief circuit judge, and judges visiting from other federal courts. The parties—and occasionally other interested groups, called "amici curiae," or "friends of the court"—submit written arguments called **briefs**. The judges consider the briefs, sometimes hear oral arguments, and then issue an opinion deciding the case. Concurring and dissenting opinions are permissible but rare: more than 90 percent of federal appellate decisions are unanimous.

Parties who lose in a federal court of appeals (and are not ready to give up and accept the judgment) have two choices. They can go directly to the Supreme Court and ask that Court to hear the case. Or they might choose to ask the same court of appeals to rehear the case **en banc** (or, in older cases, "in banc" or "in bank"), that is, as a whole court. If the circuit takes the unusual step of granting this request, all the judges sit together to decide the case. Circuits with more than 15 judges may opt to have fewer than all the judges sit for en banc hearings: for example, in the Ninth Circuit, which consists of 29 judges, the chief judge plus ten randomly chosen judges hear a case en banc.

Above the intermediate appellate courts are the highest appellate courts, sometimes referred to as "courts of last resort" or "high courts." For the moment, put aside the highest court in the federal system, the U.S. Supreme Court. Each state and territory has a court of last resort (or, in the case of Texas, two courts of last resort, one for civil cases and one for criminal cases) even though some do not have an intermediate appellate court. Some of these state high courts have only limited jurisdiction, some have discretionary (or partially discretionary) jurisdiction, and some have mandatory jurisdiction and must therefore hear every case that is appealed to them. The state courts of last resort are the final arbiters and interpreters of state law.

The United States Supreme Court

Finally, we come to the court with which you are already familiar: the **United States Supreme Court**. The Supreme Court has jurisdiction over all cases from the U.S. courts of appeals, and over some cases coming from the highest courts of the states and territories. As you probably know, the Court consists of one Chief Justice and eight Associate Justices. Like all judges authorized by Article III of the Constitution, Justices are nominated by the president and confirmed by the Senate.

Unlike the courts of appeals, most of the Supreme Court's jurisdiction is discretionary: the Court generally sets its own agenda, choosing which cases to hear. Parties dissatisfied with a ruling from the court of appeals (or the state's highest court, if the case is one over which the Supreme Court has jurisdiction) must petition the Supreme Court for a **writ of certiorari** (often shortened to "cert." and pronounced "surt"). The party challenging the lower court's ruling is called the **petitioner** (rather than the appellant), and the party responding is the **respondent** (not the appellee). If the Justices grant cert., they will hear and decide the case. If they deny cert., then the case is over and the lower court ruling stands.

About 10,000 petitions are filed every year, but fewer than 100 are granted. The media often report that the Court "refused to disturb" or "let stand" a lower court decision; usually this means that the Court denied cert.

There are two significant exceptions to this normal process (remember, as always, there are also minor variations). First, a handful of federal statutes provide for mandatory Supreme Court jurisdiction. In cases governed by those statutes, if a party chooses to appeal to the Supreme Court, the Court *must* hear and decide the case. Finally, the Court has original, mandatory jurisdiction over some types of suits, most importantly those that involve disputes between states. These cases are filed initially in the Supreme Court and do not go through the lower courts at all. Both exceptions account for a very small number of cases heard by the Justices—in some years, none.

	Who started it?	Who responds?	What happens?
CIVIL LAWSUIT	**Plaintiff** brings suit in a "complaint" ("P" or "Π").	**Defendant** defends ("D" or "Δ").	Losing defendant is **liable.**
CRIMINAL PROSECUTION	**Prosecutor** brings charge.	**Defendant** defends.	Losing defendant is **guilty** (criminally liable).
APPEALS TO HIGHER COURT	**Appellant** appeals unfavorable result to appellate court.	**Appellee** responds.	Lower court is **affirmed** or **reversed** or **vacated.**

Parties + Process

Navigating the Courts

Now that you know the structure and some details about each type of court, let's put it all together. The basic structure of the American judiciary is made up of two lines of courts: a federal hierarchy and a separate hierarchy for each state. For questions of federal law (including statutes, regulations, and the Constitution), the U.S. Supreme Court is the final word for all courts. Thus the U.S. Supreme Court is sometimes but not always the last court in every jurisdiction, state and federal.

Because we have all these different courts deciding cases, we must answer two further questions:

1. Each court must follow the decisions (or **precedent**) of courts above it—but exactly which courts' precedents count (or are **binding** or **controlling**)?
2. How do we resolve complications that arise because there are two lines of courts rather than just one?

The answer to the first question is easy. Think of each state or territory, and each region covered by a U.S. court of appeals, as a separate system. A court *must* follow the precedent of the courts that have the power to review its decision in the case. So, a federal district court in Tennessee has to follow the precedents from the U.S. Court of Appeals for the Sixth Circuit and from the U.S. Supreme Court—and nothing else. A state trial court in Tennessee (a circuit or chancery court) must follow the precedents of the Tennessee Court of Appeals (or Court of Criminal Appeals for criminal cases), the Tennessee Supreme Court, and the U.S. Supreme Court—and nothing else. And state courts must follow U.S. Supreme Court precedent only on *federal* law; the state supreme court is the final decision maker when it comes to *state* law. Of course, a court may *choose* to follow decisions of any other court if it finds those decisions persuasive, but it is not required to do so—such decisions have **persuasive authority**.

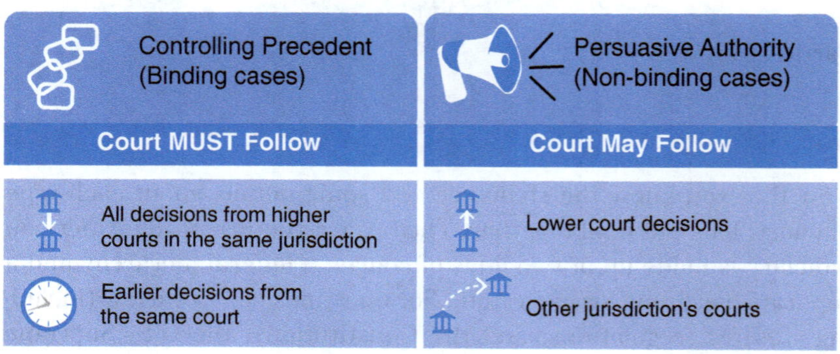

Binding Precedent

Test Your Understanding

Relying on the graphics presented thus far, list the sources of binding precedent for each of the following courts:

New York Supreme Court
California Supreme Court
U.S. District Court for the Eastern District of California
U.S. Court of Appeals for the Second Circuit

The interactions among the federal courts and the multiple state courts give rise to all sorts of complications. How does a lawyer know whether to bring a case in state court or federal court? In which of the 50+ state and territorial courts or the 94 federal district courts can it be brought? Can lawsuits move between the two systems? If the parties have already litigated in one court system, can they relitigate in another? Does the source of law governing the dispute change with the location of the chosen court? You will learn the answers to some of these questions in your Civil Procedure course. Others are the subject of at least two entire upper-class courses, Federal Courts (or Federal Jurisdiction) and Conflict of Laws. For now, you need be aware only that these important questions exist.

LITIGATION: MYTH AND REALITY

When you think about being a lawyer, what do you imagine? You may see yourself in a courtroom, prying information out of a reluctant witness and convincing a rapt jury of the rightness of your client's cause. Your primary skills are cleverness and oratory, as well as an encyclopedic knowledge of the law.

Think again. Many lawyers never try a case. And even for those who do, real civil litigation doesn't match this iconic image. Start with the fact that people who used to call themselves "trial lawyers" now call themselves "litigators." Why? Because trials are extremely rare (and juries even rarer), and most of the work of litigation happens outside a courtroom.

The Vanishing Jury Trial and the Focus on the Pretrial Phase

Most disputes are resolved before they ever get to the point of someone filing a lawsuit; studies suggest that only 8 to 12 percent of disputes with possible legal merit result in a lawsuit at all. The injured party might ignore the wrong or be unaware that it is actionable. Or the parties might resolve the dispute among themselves without filing a lawsuit, perhaps with the help of lawyers or perhaps by submitting it to outside arbitration or mediation—to which they might have agreed in advance. And even when a lawsuit is filed, most cases settle or are dismissed before trial. In the federal courts, less than 1 percent of civil lawsuits end in a trial.

Civil lawsuits end before trial because the parties reach an agreement settling the claims or the court dismisses the case as lacking merit. If the case is not dismissed or settled quickly, the case goes into the pretrial phase. During pretrial, the parties obtain more evidence from each other, from third parties, and from other sources through their own investigations (a process called "discovery"), and the judge might also make rulings about the ultimate scope of the trial, including what legal issues are at stake, what evidence will be admitted, and so on. Parties will often settle as a result of information obtained during pretrial discovery or as a result of pretrial rulings. Sometimes the pretrial phase is so long and costly that one party decides the case is not worth the expense or effort, and accepts a settlement for that reason. Judges may encourage settlement, either through their own efforts or by suggesting arbitration or mediation by a neutral third party. The judge also has authority to dismiss the case at any time for procedural defects—such as lack of jurisdiction—or may issue a judgment in favor of one party because the evidence is so lopsided that no reasonable jury could ever rule for the other party.

Finally, of the small percentage of cases that go to trial, only about two-thirds are tried before a jury. The rest are tried before a judge alone, either because the parties have no legal right to a jury trial or because the parties agree to try the case before a judge instead of a jury.

You might find all of this surprising. Aside from the prevalence of settlement, the phenomenon of the "vanishing jury" is also inconsistent with our mythical picture of litigation. In the American adversarial system, judges are supposed to decide questions of law, and juries are supposed to decide questions of fact (the distinction between questions of law and questions of fact is described in detail in Chapter 2). But this is an oversimplification: judges have more power than you might think to structure or encourage negotiations and settlement, to manage and dismiss cases, and even to try cases without a jury. You will learn more details in Civil Procedure and in Criminal Procedure (which is usually an upper-class elective), but for now, you should just use this information to modify your image of what it means to be a lawyer.

What do litigators do if they don't try cases? They are essentially problem solvers: they devise and constantly revise a strategy to obtain the best possible result for their clients. From structuring the initial lawsuit, to negotiating, to running the discovery process, to making legal arguments in front of the judge, good lawyers always keep in mind how their actions will improve the chances of a favorable settlement. Knowing the basic rules of law is important, but thinking about how to use the law creatively to the client's advantage is even more crucial. Most cases don't turn on simple rules that make one party right and the other wrong. Good lawyers use the gaps in the law to create tactical advantages and beneficial environments for achieving their clients' goals.

Criminal litigation presents a similar picture. Most defendants plead guilty in exchange for the promise of a shorter sentence than they would receive if they were convicted at trial. In the federal system, roughly 90 percent of defendants accept a plea deal. While they try more cases than the typical civil litigator, prosecutors and defenders are also more strategists and negotiators than trial lawyers.

Remedies

Before we leave our discussion of the realities of litigation, we should briefly mention two other topics that help shape American civil litigation. First, there is the question of **remedies**. Litigation occurs because one party wants something from another party. It will help you understand the cases you read during law school, and improve your ability to assist clients, if you can match the legally available remedies to the parties' needs and desires as closely as possible.

You should also be careful to separate rights (and wrongs) from remedies: a plaintiff whose rights have been violated (or whom a defendant has wronged in some other way that makes the defendant "liable") is not necessarily entitled to any particular remedy—or even any remedy at all.

Two sorts of remedies are legally available: **monetary** and **equitable**. A monetary remedy, usually called **damages**, is a remedy at law (or a "legal remedy"). An equitable remedy is a judgment from the court ordering someone to do something other than pay money (or to refrain from doing something). For example, a court might order a party to turn over a disputed item of personal property, or not to build a fence too close to a neighbor's property, or to refrain from interfering with a planned parade.

Damages come in four different varieties:

- **Compensatory (or actual) damages.** This is money to compensate the plaintiff for an injury. It can compensate for a financial loss or expenditure, or for physical or emotional pain and suffering. But it is always tied in some way to real harm.
- **Statutory damages.** Some statutes provide that a losing defendant must pay the plaintiff a set amount for each proven violation of the statute. Statutory-damage provisions are most often included in statutes when the actual damages are very low and the legislature wants to set a higher amount in order to deter potential defendants who might otherwise view the actual damages as simply part of the cost of doing business.
- **Nominal damages.** Where the plaintiff has suffered no compensable harm, a court can award a minimal amount—usually \$1—for its symbolic value. The plaintiff's harm cannot be compensated either because the plaintiff failed to prove actual damages or because the injury itself was symbolic (as is the case for some constitutional claims).
- **Punitive damages.** On top of awarding any of the other types of damages, in some circumstances a judge or jury can add an amount designed to punish the defendant (and deter future potential defendants) rather than to compensate the plaintiff. Punitive damages are often controversial and are limited by the Constitution, statutes, and common law.

Damages of some sort are almost always an available option. Whatever the injury, a plaintiff can usually ask for monetary compensation. But monetary remedies have three possible drawbacks. First, the injured party bears the burden of proving the amount of loss, and that may be difficult. Second, damages can sometimes be difficult to collect: the defendant may be bankrupt (or simply too poor to pay), may hide assets, or otherwise try to avoid paying the judgment. This latter situation arises most commonly if the judgment is from one jurisdiction and the defendant's assets are in another jurisdiction; it can be complicated, and sometimes impossible, to get the courts of one state or nation to enforce the judgments of another state or nation. When a plaintiff obtains a judgment awarding damages but is unable to actually collect the money, the defendant is said to be "judgment proof." Defendants may prove to be judgment proof because they have insufficient money, inadequate insurance, or assets that are beyond reach (perhaps in another country). Knowing in advance that a particular defendant is likely to be judgment proof helps lawyers structure the lawsuit to make sure it includes at least one defendant who is *not* judgment proof.

Finally, even if a plaintiff can prove and collect damages, money may be inadequate because of the nature of the harm. If you fail to pay your credit card bill, the credit card company will be happy with a judgment ordering you to pay the past-due amount (plus interest!). But if your former roommate takes your great-grandfather's gold wedding ring on moving out, you may not be satisfied with getting the monetary value of the ring: you want the ring itself because it is unique and cannot be replaced by purchasing another ring. Works of art are similarly unique.

That's when equitable relief is useful; in this case, it would take the form of an **injunction** ordering the roommate to return the ring (or artwork). It, too, has drawbacks, however. Sometimes, it is not possible to order the defendant to perform; if the roommate has already melted down the ring, there isn't much a court can do. Also, courts will rarely order equitable relief if it involves the performance of a promised personal service. Finally, there are times when neither monetary nor equitable relief is true compensation, but it's the best a court can do. If you drive recklessly and permanently disable a pedestrian, money will never be enough to compensate your victim, nor is there any satisfactory equitable relief. In these situations, lawyers should recognize the limited utility of the law and do the best they can. Sometimes urging your client to sincerely apologize is part of your job.

Financing Litigation

The final and perhaps most complicated litigation topic involves how lawsuits are financed. As you can already see, litigation is complex, multifaceted, and expensive. In general, lawyers—like everyone else—will not spend the enormous amounts of time and energy required by most lawsuits unless they know they will be compensated for their work. There are also additional costs associated with filing a lawsuit and conducting discovery, to say nothing of a trial. So, who pays for litigation?

In many countries, the loser pays the legal expenses (including the lawyers' fees) of the winner. By contrast, under what has come to be known as the **American Rule**, each party bears its own expenses. Think about the incentives that this provides to potential parties:

- Plaintiffs with probable-winning cases are *less* likely to file them under the American Rule than under loser-pays rules because they know that they have to pay their own legal fees even if they win. Litigation expenses, especially for complex claims or small ones, may be greater than the value of the claim.
- Plaintiffs with probable-losing cases are *more* likely to file them under the American Rule than under loser-pays rules because they know that they will not have to pay their opponents' legal fees if they lose. Plaintiffs can also calculate the effect of the American Rule on defendants and anticipate obtaining settlements even in losing cases, further increasing the incentives to file them (defendants in cases that a plaintiff is likely to win can also engage in this behavior).
- Both plaintiffs and defendants face incentives to make the litigation as expensive as possible for their opponents, especially if there is a disparity in wealth between the parties. Ethical rules should mitigate the effect of incentives to do so unfairly.

As you can see, the economic incentives are complex and interactive. Those who study the legal system cannot agree on how they operate in actual cases. People also have noneconomic reasons for filing or defending lawsuits, including reputation and vindication. And of course, most suits are not easily categorized as winning or losing at the outset, further complicating the parties' incentives. But the American Rule is clearly one driving force behind the shape of American litigation, and you should think about the incentives it creates.

Unsurprisingly, there are various rules and practices that help to mitigate some of the problematic aspects of the American Rule. We can separate the problems into two groups: those that cause too much (or too aggressive) litigation, and those that cause too little litigation. As for the first group, you will learn in Civil Procedure and in an upper-class course on Professional Responsibility that lawyers have ethical obligations that prohibit some of this sort of behavior. Whether these obligations go far enough, or are sufficiently enforced, is much disputed.

The more interesting question is what to do about plaintiffs with meritorious cases who are deterred from bringing suit because of the cost of litigation. We can identify three different solutions, each of which has been adopted in some circumstances.

First, Congress (or a state legislature) has sometimes altered the American Rule by statute, providing that a winning plaintiff can recover litigation expenses from the defendant. The most common example is antidiscrimination and other civil rights claims. In those types of cases, the judge has the authority to require the losing party to pay the winning party's "reasonable attorneys' fees." The Supreme Court has interpreted these provisions as essentially requiring the award of expenses to a winning plaintiff, but allowing an award to a prevailing defendant only if the plaintiff's suit was frivolous. Plaintiffs are thus encouraged to bring close, difficult, or novel cases because as long as the claim has some merit, the plaintiff will not have to pay defendant's attorneys' fees, even if the plaintiff loses. Congress has made the judgment that society is better off with more, rather than fewer, civil rights cases, even if not all of them turn out to be winners.

Second, in many cases lawyers and clients agree that the lawyers' fees will be a percentage of what the plaintiff wins rather than a flat or hourly charge. If the plaintiff loses, the lawyer does not get paid. This is known as a **contingency fee** and is most common in tort cases. The usual contingency fee is about one-third of the plaintiff's recovery. This arrangement encourages lawyers to evaluate carefully the likelihood of winning, and the likely amount of damages, in order to determine whether the case is worth their while. It therefore encourages the filing of meritorious suits and discourages the filing of nonmeritorious ones.

But contingency fees do not solve the problem for plaintiffs whose expected winnings are small in amount or who seek something other than monetary compensation; the litigation expenses will still be large, but the lawyer will have no incentive to take the case. The third solution is designed for just such a situation. Sometimes, a defendant will act in a way that causes a little damage to a lot of people. Perhaps a credit card company overcharges on interest, so that a million people are each overcharged \$10 or \$15, or two airlines illegally conspire to raise ticket prices by \$5 a ticket. It will not be worth any lawyer's time to take an individual client's suit. But there are various ways that the suits can be consolidated. The most important method of consolidation is for one (or a few) plaintiffs to bring a **class action**, in which they are representing the entire class of people who were harmed by the same defendant in the same way. There are also other methods of consolidation, usually covered in an upper-class course in Complex Litigation. And for all consolidated cases, there are various ways to pay the lawyers: they might get a percentage of the total recovery (\$10-15 million, in our first example) or they might get court-ordered attorneys' fees paid by the defendant. Again, most of these cases settle, but the availability of consolidation is what allows them to be brought in the first place.

Despite the ethical constraints on too much litigation and the three solutions to the problem of too little litigation, the American Rule still exerts an influence on American litigation—and lawyers, judges, and scholars still debate its merits.

So far, we have covered essential background for your first-year classes—but that's not enough. With the next chapter, we begin to focus more directly on the legal concepts and tools that you will be using in your first year and throughout your legal education.

Chapter 5

FUNDAMENTAL LEGAL CONCEPTS

Lawyers use specialized terms and classifications to understand complex ideas and to communicate them to others. This legal lingo can be difficult to learn, but at some point, you will discover that you have started to "think (and speak) like a lawyer." In this chapter, we introduce key concepts that will aid you in thinking and speaking like a lawyer. These concepts apply across a broad range of legal doctrines. They are therefore relevant to every one of your first-year courses. These concepts are the tools that lawyers use to analyze, argue, and apply legal doctrines. You must be familiar with them in order to fully understand your assignments and class discussions. This chapter introduces you to these concepts, many of which will be further explored in your courses throughout law school.

In order to help you to understand the many concepts that we introduce, we arrange them based on shared characteristics. The first set of terms includes dichotomies, or attempts to divide the world into two complementary categories. The second set includes cross-cutting legal doctrines: legal rules that apply in many different legal areas. The third set has developed from the application of economic principles to legal questions. The fourth set resists categorization except that all of the terms are used regularly, and none fit into the three categories.

DICHOTOMIES

Dichotomies drive legal analysis. Lawyers often make arguments that depend on comparing or contrasting things based on their differences, such as arguing that a rule from one case should not apply in another. Some differences do not matter: whether a case is argued on a Tuesday or a Thursday, or by a male or female lawyer, should not affect our examination of the legal issues. But whether a case is argued in a Kansas or Missouri court *does* matter because those courts are bound by different precedent (as we discuss in Chapter 4). Knowing what sorts of differences matter, and how, allows lawyers and judges to focus their analyses and arguments. In Chapter 2, we introduced two important dichotomies: law versus fact and substance versus procedure. In this section, we address three other important and common legal dichotomies: rules versus standards, categorization versus balancing, and objective versus subjective conditions.

We address each of these dichotomies in more detail below, but it might help you to have a brief overview. The distinction between **rules** and **standards** goes to the form that governing law takes. Law may take the form of a rule (a clear and rigid mandate) or of a standard (a fuzzy and flexible criterion). Our second dichotomy is one particularly common form of the rule/standard distinction: **categorization** tests, which are rules, and **balancing** tests, which are standards. Courts use categorization and balancing tests to aid them in making decisions. Finally, the law may be concerned with **objective conditions** (external to any particular individual) or **subjective conditions** (what a particular individual actually means or believes).

Rules versus Standards

Law may take the form of a rule or of a standard. **Rules** give the decision-maker as little discretion as possible. **Standards** give the decision-maker more discretion and less guidance. (We are here using "rules" in a very narrow sense, as the opposite of "standards." Be careful: all legal doctrine might be described as "rules" in the broad sense, as used in the phrases "rules of law" or the "rules of the game.") The requirement that drivers drive at or below the posted speed limit is a *rule* in traffic law—drivers do not have the discretion to drive faster if they determine it would be safe to do so. By contrast, the requirement that drivers leave a safe distance between their car and the car in front of them is a *standard*—drivers determine what "safety" requires based on the conditions of the road and the speed at which they are driving.

How can you distinguish rules from standards? Standards usually contain words that require a contextual determination or a judgment call—look for words like "reasonable," "important," or "safe." Rules, on the other hand, operate automatically once the predicate facts are determined, such as a posted speed limit of 65 miles per hour. That doesn't mean that rules are always easy to apply: they may have multiple exceptions that identify circumstances in which an otherwise applicable rule will not apply for some reason. For example, icy roads may be an exception to the top speed of 65, requiring drivers to slow down. Ultimately, though, the idea behind a rule (and its rule-bound exceptions) is to reduce the decision to a mechanical judgment.

Test Your Understanding

Here are three rules of contract law (here we are using "rule" in the broader sense of a doctrine or law). Decide whether each is more like a rule (in the narrower sense) or a standard.

1. A valid contract between two parties will be enforced unless it is against public policy.
2. A contract that cannot be completed within a year will not be enforced unless it is in writing.
3. A contract is not enforceable against a person under 18 years of age.

Standards have been likened to mud and rules to crystals. This commonly used metaphor can be helpful in thinking about their differences. But keep in mind that the difference in practice may not always be so sharp. Many laws lie somewhere along the continuum between the most crystal-clear rule and the muddiest standard. The more exceptions a rule has, the more likely it is to operate like a standard. And even where a doctrine clearly starts out as a rule or a standard, it might evolve into the other—in particular, as we show a little later, rules often turn into standards.

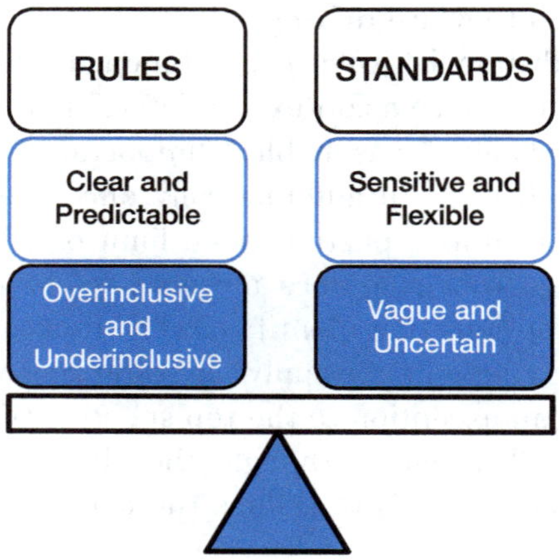

Rules versus Standards

To make all this concrete, let's focus on a specific standard: a requirement that homeowners take "reasonable" care to prevent items on their property from causing harm to others. Imagine that Nathan, a homeowner, puts a metal garbage can in his driveway on the day that the garbage trucks are coming around. We might think that he acted reasonably—even if the garbage can accidentally tips over in an unexpected storm and rolls into the street, causing damage. But imagine a different homeowner, Russell, who puts a pile of dynamite in his driveway: that is probably *not* reasonable behavior. If the applicable law holds people liable for harms if and only if they acted unreasonably, Nathan will probably not be liable for damage caused by the garbage can, but Russell will probably be liable for damage caused by the dynamite.

Because of the uncertainty inherent in standards, some judges express a preference for clear and certain rules. But rules have their own disadvantages. An effective way to appreciate the differences between rules and standards is to compare their advantages and disadvantages. To do this, try to formulate a *rule* that will make Russell liable for damages that occur when the dynamite in front of his house explodes, but will not make Nathan liable for damages when his garbage can rolls into the street and damages a parked car.

Now compare your rule to the "reasonable care" standard. The primary disadvantage of rules is that they are often both over- and underinclusive. You probably came up with some version of a rule that specifically prohibits leaving dynamite in a driveway. But that rule will not impose liability on someone who leaves a loaded gun in the driveway—and it would be impossible to list all of the potentially dangerous items that should result in liability. At the same time, there might be a situation in which placing dynamite in a driveway is reasonable: for example, if the house is in the process of demolition. If we apply the no-dynamite rule strictly, the result will be unfair. The careful demolitions expert will be held liable, but the irresponsible gun owner will not.

If we begin by banning dynamite and gradually add other items, we might partially solve the problem. As the list grows, however, courts will have to figure out how and why to add other items. They will probably come up with a principle such as "no dangerous objects may be left unattended in the driveway" (or perhaps the rule will start out that way, rather than as a specific dynamite ban). But as soon as we insert "no dangerous objects," we leave the judge discretion to determine which objects are dangerous and which are not. And because some objects might be dangerous in some situations but not in others, and because in some situations there may be good reasons to use dangerous objects, we are likely to end up with a law that bans *unreasonably* dangerous objects. For these reasons, doctrines that start out as rules often tend to morph into standards. It is hard to maintain a clear rule in the face of ever-changing factual contexts and a desire to achieve fair and just results.

Test Your Understanding

Imagine that a professor wants to adopt a policy that creates a strong incentive for students to attend every class by penalizing students who miss class and by rewarding students who attend class.

1. Begin by formulating a clear and predictable rule for the professor's attendance policy that leaves nothing to student interpretation or debate (you might think about grade adjustments, for example).
2. Now apply your rule to Ben, who consistently comes to class late, attending for only the last 5 or 10 minutes of a 50-minute class.
3. Now apply your rule to Jonathan, who misses several classes because of a contagious illness.
4. Change your rule (but keep it a rule, not a standard) to deal fairly with Ben and Jonathan.
5. Now apply your new rule to Elizabeth, a student who misses class because of a car accident, and to Sarah, a student who often arrives a minute or two late.
6. Devise either a new rule or a standard to deal fairly with all the students described so far, and with any others you can imagine. Explain why you prefer either a rule or a standard.

You should notice that standards such as "reasonableness" are exactly the sort of legal doctrines that make students uncomfortable. Standards are uncertain and indefinite because there are no mechanical tests for determining whether something is reasonable. At the same time, however, a standard is not infinitely malleable, as the dynamite example shows (or if you don't like dynamite, you can substitute wild animals, loaded guns, or anything else you consider unreasonably dangerous). The more cases you read, the better you will be able to determine what behavior is reasonable in any situation—but there will always be surprises!

Categorization versus Balancing

The rules-versus-standards dichotomy is broad and general. The distinction may be easier to understand by focusing on the most common example of that dichotomy: **categorization tests** versus **balancing tests**. Generally speaking, categorization tests are more like rules, while balancing tests are more like standards.

Categorization tests typically take the form "where *a* is true, then *y* result follows; where *b* is true, then *z* result follows." All of the action takes place in determining whether the situation is in category *a* or *b*. So, for example, you will learn in your Constitutional Law class that if the government draws distinctions based on race, they will almost always be unconstitutional; but if the government draws distinctions based on age, they will almost always be constitutional. The tests are structured to allow very little discretion once the court decides whether the distinction is based on race or age.

Balancing tests, on the other hand, direct a court to consider various factors to determine the correct legal answer. In Civil Procedure, you will learn that one part of the test for whether a court can exercise authority (or "personal jurisdiction") over a particular defendant is whether doing so is consistent with "traditional notions of fair play and substantial justice." In applying this standard, the court takes into account the interests of the plaintiff, of the defendant, of the state in which the court is located, and of the judicial system as a whole. These various interests are to be weighed against each other. Hence, tests like this are referred to as "balancing tests" because the judge places factors that favor one outcome on one side of a figurative balancing scale and those that favor the opposite outcome on the other side. The judge's decision is based on which side weighs more. You can see that balancing tests give the court a great deal more discretion than categorization tests do.

It is not always easy to tell the difference between categorization and balancing, and tests are sometimes an amalgam of the two. Government discrimination, as we noted above, is evaluated using a categorization test that treats the basis of the discrimination—race or age, for example—as a category that dictates whether the discrimination is constitutional or not. But some categories do not dictate such a clear test: if the court concludes the discrimination is based on sex, then it must determine whether sex-based distinctions are "substantially related" to an "important" state interest—which looks like a classic balancing test. Or take the other part of the test for personal jurisdiction: a court cannot exercise jurisdiction over someone who lacks "minimum contacts" with the specific state in which the court sits. That sounds like a categorization, but there is a lot of discretion in determining whether the threshold has been reached. A court will have to balance the level of "contacts" against the fairness of dragging the defendant to the particular state: if the defendant visited the state just once, long ago and unconnected with the subject matter of the lawsuit, a court would be unlikely to find the requirement satisfied.

When you read a case, try to figure out whether it is applying rules or standards, categorization tests or balancing tests, or some combination. Why should you care whether a court is categorizing or balancing? Because it affects the meaning and implications of the court's decision. If you are asked in class (as you inevitably will be) how to resolve a hypothetical case similar to one assigned, your answer will depend, in part, on the nature of the test used by the court. If the applicable legal doctrine uses categorization tests, you will have to start by determining into which category the hypothetical facts fall (you should *not* begin by making arguments about why it would be wrong or unfair to reach a particular result). For balancing tests, you will start by identifying the factors that should be considered on the balancing scale. These dichotomies are crucial to the work of attorneys, who often engage in the task of anticipating how the law will treat some action or arguing how some event should be treated in light of existing doctrine. One way to approach the task of distinguishing between categorization tests and balancing tests (or between rules and standards) is to ask how much discretion the court has: the more discretion, the more standard-like the test.

Test Your Understanding

You have been asked to draft a law that would protect people from injury (to person or property) caused by items left by a homeowner in her driveway but also allows her to use her driveway in the usual way. Draft a version of the law as a categorization test. Draft a version that includes a balancing test. What are the tradeoffs presented by your draft laws?

Objective versus Subjective.

Objective standards are external: does the person's behavior—carrying so many heavy boxes—seem risky to outsiders?

Subjective standards are internal: does the person think that carrying so many heavy boxes is risky?

Objective versus Subjective

Our last dichotomy relates to two different types of standards: **objective** versus **subjective**. **Subjective standards** depend on internal conditions—a person's specific intentions and beliefs. **Objective standards** depend on external conditions—factors external to the person. Almost any legal evaluation of a person's actions will turn on subjective or objective evidence, or some combination of both.

Subjective standards focus on the individual. **Good faith**, for example, is a subjective standard: people are judged by whether they *believed* that what they did was appropriate or that a representation that they made was true. Sometimes a person's good faith is referred to as a "bona fide" belief or honesty-in-fact. Other subjective standards might turn on whether individuals had particular knowledge, whether they intended a particular consequence, or what their motives were. Each standard pays attention to the person's thoughts and individual characteristics.

Objective standards focus on the world. **Reasonableness** is an example of an objective standard: it asks what should be considered appropriate given the circumstances, regardless of what the particular person herself thought or intended. In tort law, for example, liability is often measured by whether a hypothetical person exercising the appropriate amount of care would have done what the defendant did. We saw earlier that leaving a garbage can in the driveway is probably reasonable, but leaving dynamite in the same place is probably not reasonable. In contract law, whether a communication constitutes an offer is based on what a reasonable person in the position of the offeree would have thought. Reasonableness standards are pervasive in law, arising in nearly every subject (including all of your first-year courses). Such standards often require a judge to look at "the totality of the circumstances" to determine if an action was reasonable. Any legal test that does not depend on a person's state of mind is an objective test.

CROSS-CUTTING LEGAL DOCTRINES

In your 1L courses, you will study legal doctrines that govern particular subjects, such as torts, contracts, and crimes. A few doctrines, however, cut across subjects. These cross-cutting doctrines are relevant in multiple subject areas, although the details might vary depending on context. You might think that *every* 1L course in which the doctrine is relevant would discuss these doctrines, but the reverse is often true: each of your first-year teachers will assume you have learned the doctrine in another course, and therefore none will cover it in any detail! Learning about these doctrines now will help to address that problem, improving your understanding of the material assigned and increasing your confidence in class. In this section, we discuss four particularly common cross-cutting doctrines: states of mind, precedent and stare decisis, burdens of proof, and standards of review.

States of Mind

Legal rules determine the legal consequences of particular acts. Unlike natural consequences, however, legal consequences usually vary with an individual's **state of mind.** If you throw a rock at a window, the window will break regardless of whether you threw it at the window on purpose, you threw it at an escaping burglar and it hit the window, or you threw it as the result of an involuntary muscle spasm. Your legal responsibility (or liability or culpability) for the broken window, however, might depend on your state of mind. A person might be liable (in civil contexts) or culpable (in criminal contexts) for intentional conduct, knowing conduct, reckless conduct, negligent conduct, or all conduct regardless of state of mind. Be sure you know which state of mind must be proven in the particular context you are considering. Your courses will fill in the detailed description of each state of mind, but here is a short summary.

- Intentional or purposeful. The actor intends the consequences of the actions. Depending on the context, this might simply mean an intention to take the action, or an intention to accomplish a particular goal by taking the action.
- Knowing. The actor is aware that the actions will almost certainly lead to particular consequences.
- Reckless. The actor consciously disregards a substantial risk that particular consequences will occur.
- Negligent. The actor does not take reasonable care to avoid the consequences of the actions.
- Strict liability. The law does not care what the actor intends or what care is taken, but imposes liability for all consequences of the actions.

You can see the lines between the different states of mind by considering the case of an accident in which a driver Jermaine has hit and injured a pedestrian Mallika. Jermaine's actions would be considered *intentional* if he *meant* to hit the pedestrian—for example, if he was angry at the pedestrian and wanted to hurt her. The driver's actions would be considered *knowing* if Jermaine sees Mallika crossing the street in front of his car but does not slow down because he is in a hurry to get somewhere; although Jermaine has no particular hostility toward Mallika and therefore does not intend to hurt her, Jermaine knows that he will almost certainly hit her. Jermaine's actions would be considered *reckless* if he gets into the car knowing that he is too drunk to drive, or is driving without lights after dark, or is taking any other action that is substantially likely to cause harm. Jermaine's actions would be considered *negligent* if he has been having intermittent problems with his brakes but has not taken the car in for service, or if he is driving faster than conditions allow, or is taking any other action that a reasonable person would not take. Jermaine would be held *strictly liable* only if the legislature (or a judicial decision) specifies that anyone taking a particular action (driving in a park, driving between 3 a.m. and 5 a.m., driving across a road that is closed off for a parade, etc.) is liable for all harms caused.

Test Your Understanding

Use the dichotomies to evaluate the five states of mind. Which states of mind are objective? Which states of mind are subjective? Which states of mind are standards? Which are rules?

Precedent and Stare Decisis

In a common law system, previously decided cases are an important source of authority. These decisions are known as **precedent**. Courts must follow the decisions announced by courts above them in the judicial hierarchy. In the federal system, U.S. courts of appeals must follow the decisions of the U.S. Supreme Court. U.S. district courts must follow the decisions of the Supreme Court and of the court of appeals for the circuit where the district is located. Florida, for example, is in the Eleventh Circuit, and its three district courts (northern, middle, and southern) are bound by Eleventh Circuit precedent (we discussed the judicial hierarchies in more detail in Chapter 4). Higher courts' decisions constitute **binding precedent**. Decisions issued by courts at the same level, or below, in the hierarchy (or any court in a different hierarchy) are not controlling (binding) but may be persuasive. A district judge on the U.S. District Court for the Northern District of Florida deciding a question of federal law, for example, may be influenced by a decision of another district court, of a circuit other than the Eleventh, or even of a state court. All of those decisions would be **persuasive authority**, rather than controlling authority. The only way to determine whether an earlier case is binding is to trace the hierarchy: where does the current court stand in relation to the court that issued the earlier decision? (The type of law at issue matters, too. A federal court interpreting state law must defer to that state's courts on questions of the state's law.)

Tracing the line of authority is relatively straightforward, but *applying* precedential cases can be more difficult. Determining how a particular precedent—or line of precedents—actually applies to the case before the court is one of the key tasks of lawyers and judges. A new case will raise questions that share some, but not all, salient facts in common with the earlier case. Much legal analysis (and much of the discussion of precedent in judicial opinions) turns on which precedents are sufficiently similar to the facts at hand (and therefore should govern) and which are distinguishable from the facts at hand (and therefore do not control the outcome). Most of your first-year professors will spend a great deal of time spinning out hypothetical fact situations designed to test the reach of the precedents that you have read. This is where the analogical reasoning we discuss in Chapter 2 becomes crucially important!

Courts are obligated to follow the decisions of superior courts, but what about their *own* prior decisions? The principle of **stare decisis** (pronounced star-ē de-cī-sis and roughly translated as "stand by what has been decided") directs courts to also follow their own precedent rather than overruling it. It is a presumption rather than a command: stare decisis requires a court to have a very good reason for changing its position on a legal issue. Because of the pull of stare decisis, good lawyers faced with bad precedent try to distinguish the old ruling rather than urge that the earlier case was wrongly decided and should be overruled. Once again, a lawyer's task is to explain why one case should (or should not) govern another, and, once again, analogical reasoning is the key.

Test Your Understanding

A federal statute punishes anyone who "carries a gun during the commission of a felony." The U.S. Supreme Court has already held that keeping a gun in the glove compartment of a vehicle while conducting a drug deal in the vehicle counts as "carrying" a gun in the commission of a felony. Is keeping a gun in the trunk of a car while conducting a drug deal "carrying" it for purposes of the statute? Is the trunk case governed by the glove-compartment case, or is it distinguishable? What arguments would you make, and what reasoning would you hope to find in the glove-compartment case to support your arguments?

Burdens of Proof

The **burden of proof** assigns responsibility to a one party to prove a disputed fact or claim. It includes the **burden of production** (introduce enough evidence), and the **burden of persuasion** (convince the fact finder to view the facts in the manner supportive of the party's position). In litigation, the burden is typically on the plaintiff in a civil suit and on the prosecutor in a criminal case. If the party bearing the burden of proof does not meet the burden by presenting a sufficiently persuasive case, the other party automatically wins. Statutes sometimes change these allocations. Knowing who has the burden of proof is most important in close cases: ties go to the party *without* the burden.

A second aspect of burden of proof is the level of certainty to which the party bearing the burden must establish a fact. How certain, in other words, must the fact finder be that the fact is true? The three common standards of proof lie on a continuum of certainty.

- In order to convict the criminal defendant, the jury must be persuaded of guilt **beyond a reasonable doubt**. This is the greatest burden, and it is often described as near certainty.
- In most civil cases, the plaintiff must only persuade the fact finder that the plaintiff's claim is supported by **a preponderance of the evidence**. You can think of preponderance as requiring that the party with the burden prove that it is "more likely than not" that the party's version of events is correct. Preponderance of the evidence is the easiest standard to satisfy, requiring the least evidence.
- In a limited number of instances, the party must show a claim or fact by **clear and convincing evidence**. This standard is a middle ground, lying between preponderance and beyond a reasonable doubt.

If the probability that a fact or claim is true is 50 percent, then the evidence is in **equipoise**—the scales of proof are equally weighted—and the party with the burden loses. There is no mechanical test for determining exactly how much evidence is necessary to meet each of these standards; as you study cases that apply the different standards, you will get a feel for the general contours of each. For now, you need to understand only that these three standards are different. Be sure you know what standard is relevant in any disputed fact or claim.

Burdens of proof are relevant beyond the world of courtroom litigation. If you are drafting a contract, negotiating a settlement, or structuring a deal, you will need to know what a court will do if a dispute arises. Parties to a contract may even want to change the burden of proof that would apply if they later find themselves in disagreement. In certain circumstances, you can specify a different burden of proof in the contract itself. But to do so, you have to understand how burdens work and which would ordinarily apply.

Test Your Understanding

A trial court instructs the jury that they must find for the defendant unless the plaintiff shows the existence of a crucial fact by clear and convincing evidence. The jury finds for the plaintiff. Defendant appeals, and the appellate court holds that the trial court made an error of law in instructing the jury: the plaintiff actually needed to prove the existence of the fact by a preponderance of the evidence. The court of appeals is permitted to affirm despite a legal error, if and only if that error is harmless. Should the court of appeals affirm (agree with) the judgment for the plaintiff or send the case back (remand) for a new trial so that a new jury can be correctly instructed?

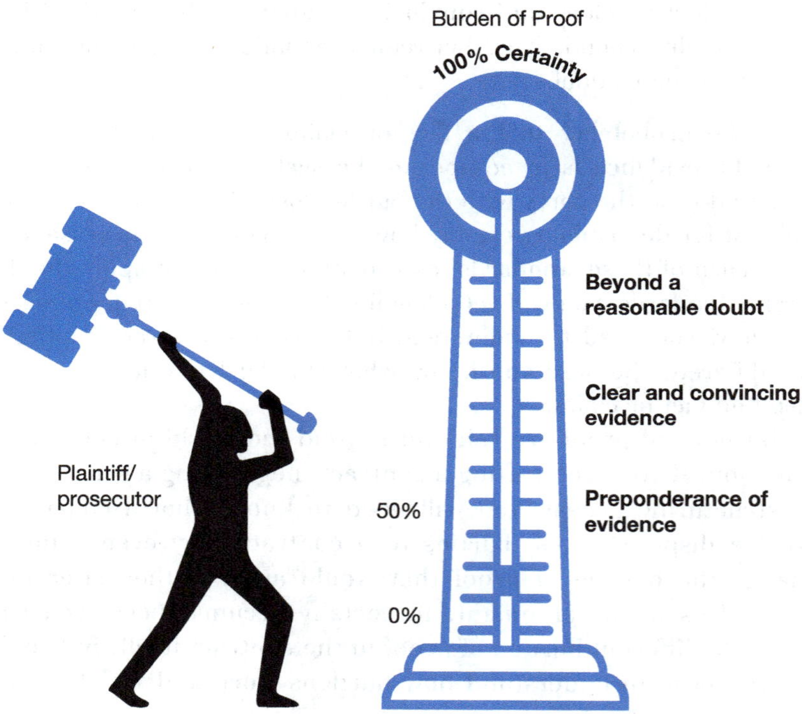

Burdens of Proof

Standards of Review

The final cross-cutting doctrine that we consider is the **standard of review.** It is common in the American legal system, as well as in others, for a person or group of people to review the determination of another person. Appellate courts review the decisions of trial courts. Judges also review agency decisions when they are challenged. The reviewer's first task is to decide how closely to scrutinize the original decision. The reviewer could undertake the entire decision-making process anew, showing no deference to the original decision-maker. Or the reviewer could treat parts of the decision-making process as complete, deferring to the original decision-maker to some extent.

In law school, most of your reading assignments will consist of the opinions of appellate courts reviewing the judgment of a lower court or other decision-maker. You will therefore have to recognize which standard of review the appellate court is using. Appellate courts employ three basic standards of review: de novo, clearly erroneous, and abuse of discretion.

Rulings on questions of law are reviewed **de novo** (meaning "from the beginning" and pronounced dē nō-vō). De novo review means that the appellate court approaches the issue as a new question, completely independent of whatever the trial court decided. If the appellate court disagrees with the trial court's interpretation of the law, it imposes its own judgment instead. This standard of review shows the least amount of deference—in fact, no deference—to the trial court.

Findings of fact, however, are reversed only if the appellate court finds that the trial court's decision was **clearly erroneous**. A decision subject to clearly erroneous review is overturned only if the appellate court is convinced that the decision cannot possibly be correct. If a reasonable judge could have reached the conclusion reached by the lower court, that conclusion is *not* clearly erroneous. This standard of review is deferential to trial courts because it treats the lower court's (or agency's) findings as probably correct. The deferential standard is based on the principle that trial courts, especially but not exclusively juries, are responsible for fact-finding.

Finally, some decisions are committed to the trial court's or agency's discretion—the trial court or agency is allowed to make whatever decision it thinks best. Such a decision can be reversed only if it is so egregiously wrong that it constitutes an **abuse of discretion**. Usually such a finding means that the court made an underlying error of law or considered illegitimate factors in exercising its discretion. This standard of review is the most deferential to trial courts.

Again, there is a continuum, with increasing deference given to the original decision-maker as the standard moves from de novo (no deference) to clearly erroneous (strong deference) to abuse of discretion (very strong deference). Review of agency decisions works similarly, with more deference given to an agency's findings of fact and less deference given to an agency's ruling on legal questions, although the terminology differs slightly.

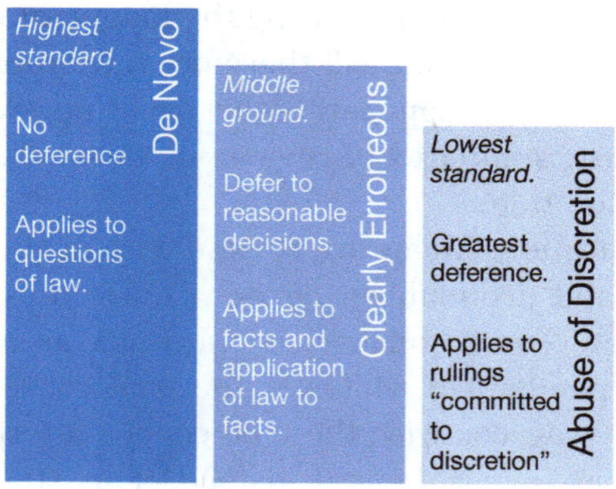

Standards of Review

Although the names of these standards are likely new to you, their operation is intuitive. Imagine that you are a parent giving your daughter money to buy a toy on an outing with her grandparents. You have set some ground rules: no guns, and nothing that makes so much noise that it will wake her younger sibling from a nap. Beyond that, your daughter may choose whatever toy she likes. She comes home with a water pistol that whistles when it shoots water. How do you decide whether to "affirm" the child's decision and let her keep the toy?

- Is the water pistol a gun? The no-guns rule is essentially a question of law, subject to de novo review: if a water pistol counts as a gun under *your* definition, the child will have to return it—it is to no avail that *she* thought you meant only guns that shot bullets.
- Is the water pistol too loud? On the question of whether the whistling will wake her sibling, the child has determined that, as a matter of fact, it will not do so. If you were acting like a court, you would have to accept her finding unless it is clearly

erroneous: for example, if she were to claim that an airhorn wouldn't wake her sibling. (Of course, most parents would not treat young children's factual determinations as entitled to too much deference—but you get the point!)

- Is the water pistol an acceptable toy? You have given her discretion to choose, so the water pistol should be fine. But if she had spent her money on a candy bar, that might constitute an abuse of her discretion to choose a *toy*.

The basic standards of review intersect in various ways. For example, consider the trial court's decision on a mixed question of law and fact. The appellate court will accept the trial court's findings of fact unless those findings are clearly erroneous. It will determine for itself whether the trial court applied the correct legal doctrine. If so, it will uphold the application of the law to the facts unless that application is clearly erroneous. Similarly, if the trial court makes an error of law in its decision, the appellate court will reverse even if the decision is committed to the court's discretion (as, in the illustration above, when the child chooses a candy bar under the erroneous assumption that it counts as a toy).

Test Your Understanding

Return to the "Test Your Understanding" exercise about Hannah and Joshua and the fence on page 44.

Recall that the trial court held:

> If a property owner does not object to another's known trespass on her property, the owner is deemed to have consented to the trespass.
>
> Joshua asked Hannah about building the fence, and Hannah did not object.
>
> Therefore, Hannah consented to the fence.

What standard of review should the appellate court apply to each of the trial court's three holdings?

Questions about precedent (and stare decisis), states of mind, burdens of proof, and standards of review will arise frequently and in every course. Without some knowledge of these concepts, you will be unable to fully comprehend your reading assignments.

INTERDISCIPLINARY CONCEPTS IN LAW

The social sciences have had a substantial impact on the law. Concepts from economics have had an especially significant effect. We focus on the economic concepts that are most influential. Law professors will use at least some of the law and economics ideas that we discuss here, and some law professors will use all of these concepts. (Note that the way these concepts are used in law may differ from how economists use them—that is, law and economics theory is not always the same as pure economic theory.) Psychology has also been a fruitful source of concepts used in legal argument, especially in response to some of the law and economics theories. Specifically, studies by psychologists have shown that people are prone to make systematic errors in their thinking called "cognitive biases." Cognitive biases prevent people from behaving in the ways predicted by economists, who assume rationality.

Law and Economics

The modern American law and economics movement can trace its roots to the 1960s, and, in particular, to the work of University of Chicago economist Ronald Coase and Yale law professor Guido Calabresi. Beginning in the 1970s, Richard Posner extended and elaborated the theoretical insights of Coase and Calabresi. Posner brought those ideas with him to the federal courts, where he served as a court of appeals judge for 36 years and wrote numerous opinions that can be found in your casebooks. The law and economics movement has been so influential that every law school has numerous scholars in the field, and virtually every law school course will borrow some concepts and insights from it. For that reason, you should be familiar with at least the following nine basic concepts.

Economic Incentives. The most basic idea from law and economics is that economic incentives influence people's behavior even when the law does not. An economic incentive is the reward provided by a market for certain behavior. Markets, of course, are composed of buyers and sellers. Markets exist for anything that people wish to exchange: goods, services, property, ideas, and so on. People's actions will be influenced by the reward—money, goods, or services—they expect to receive in return in the marketplace. If you are selling your house, for example, you can *ask* for any amount you wish, and no law will try to stop you. But you cannot charge more than a buyer is willing to pay. Thus, the real estate market creates an economic incentive to set your price at the level at which your house will sell and no higher. Although legal rules may allow sellers to ask for more money and for buyers to offer less, sellers normally can charge and buyers normally must pay only what the market will bear.

Collective Action Problems. Collective action problems are one type of market failure. Often economic incentives provided by markets will induce a beneficial change. For example, if the price of gasoline becomes too high, it might spur the development and purchase of more fuel-efficient cars or greater use of public transportation (you might think about how various laws might either encourage or discourage these trends). But sometimes the socially beneficial or "economically efficient" (see below) result will be blocked by what economists call a collective action problem. Imagine a group of neighbors who share the use of a common pond for fishing and other recreational activities. It gets contaminated by Eurasian milfoil (a virulent strain of algae that, if not removed, destroys all other life in the pond). The cost of destroying the invading algae is less than the total benefit of its removal to all the neighbors, but the cost is more than the individual benefit to any single neighbor. No individual has an incentive to pay by herself to have the algae removed, and, indeed, each would be foolish to provide her neighbors with that expensive benefit. The law—in this case, probably in the form of a neighborhood association with the power to impose a "tax" on each homeowner—must step in to solve the collective action problem.

Economic Efficiency. Many believe that a well-functioning legal system tries to attain the best results for the lowest costs. The goal of economic efficiency can shape both structural and procedural elements of a legal system, and the substantive legal doctrines that influence behavior outside the courtroom. Law and economics scholars generally are concerned with two distinct types of efficiency: Pareto efficiency and Kaldor-Hicks efficiency.

- A specific outcome or result is **Pareto optimal** or **Pareto efficient** if there is no change from that outcome that can make someone better off without making someone else worse off.
- The **Kaldor-Hicks efficiency** standard focuses on general social welfare: if the winners would end up better off even if they were to fully compensate the losers for their losses, then the rule maximizes collective well-being.

You can think of the Pareto standard as requiring that *each and every* person in society be better off (or unchanged) as a result of a legal rule, whereas the Kaldor-Hicks standard requires only that *all* persons collectively are better off. In law and economics theory, laws are tested against the ultimate goal of economic efficiency, considering all facts and circumstances related to that goal. Most economic analysis of law is based on Kaldor-Hicks efficiency.

Cost-Benefit Analysis. In order to evaluate whether a rule is economically efficient, we must calculate the costs and benefits of the rule. For example, a rule that requires people to pay for the damage they cause is likely to induce them to take greater care to avoid causing damage. The rule will be economically efficient if it causes people to take the optimum amount of care given the likelihood of damage, the cost of that damage, and the cost of taking care. We don't want to incur either the costs of too much care or the damage costs resulting from taking too little care. This type of comparison of the costs of a decision to its benefits is called, aptly, a cost-benefit analysis.

Test Your Understanding

Where should we set the speed limit? What factors should be considered? Should we abandon speed limits?

Expected Value. In weighing the costs and benefits, you will have to determine the expected value of a particular course of action.

The expected value is the amount you can expect to gain (or lose) by taking the action. Expected value takes into account the costs of a course of action, the value of the outcome (gain or loss), and the probability of that outcome. Expected value, then, is the probability (P) of an outcome (B) less costs (C): $(P \times B) - C$. Suppose, for example, a new invention—if patented—has a 50 percent probability of earning its inventor $1,000 (a patent gives the owner the *exclusive* right to manufacture and sell the invention) and a 50 percent probability of earning the inventor nothing. (We assume that the inventor has a 100 percent chance of earning nothing without a patent.) The probability times benefit $(P \times B)$ is $500 (or 50 percent of $1000). The inventor should therefore be willing to spend up to $499 to patent the invention. As long as the costs of patenting the invention are less than the probable benefits, the inventor is better off because the expected value is positive. If patenting the invention costs $600, the expected value of the patent application is negative (specifically, –$100), which counsels against going forward.

Test Your Understanding

Consider a lottery game in which you can win $50 and it costs $10 to play. Should you play if you have a 10 percent probability of winning? Should you play if you have a 50 percent probability of winning? (Remember: Expected Value $= (P \times B) - C$, where P is the probability of winning, B is the benefit or amount of the winnings, and C is the cost of playing.)

You can use expected value calculations whenever you are trying to decide whether a particular (certain or speculative) benefit is worth the (certain or speculative) cost: for example, whether a particular contract should be entered into or whether it should be enforced, whether a court should order a party to produce particular documents, or whether a particular legal rule should be adopted.

Transaction Costs. Transaction costs are those costs incurred to *undertake* an action as distinguished from the direct cost of the *action itself*. The total cost of going to a movie, for example, obviously includes the price for the ticket but also includes transaction costs such as the costs of transportation to and from the movie theater and the time spent finding out where and when the movie was playing. In deciding whether to go to a movie, you obviously should take into account both the ticket price and the transaction costs.

The Coase Theorem. In a seminal work, the economist Ronald Coase asserted that in the absence of transaction costs, any legal rule will produce a socially efficient outcome. In other words, legal rules don't affect whether socially optimal actions will be taken. The rules affect only who takes those actions.

A classic example of how the Coase Theorem works is the question of what rule should apply to property owners whose actions on their own property constitute a nuisance to their neighbors. Assume that Chloe and Elliot own adjacent property. Chloe's manufacturing plant produces pollution, which affects Elliot's property. Let's say that Chloe's pollution causes Elliot \$100 worth of damage and that it would cost \$50 for Chloe to avoid the damage to Elliot. Under those facts, the efficient result is for Chloe to avoid the damage. Why? The cost of avoiding the damage is less than the cost of the damage. Consider what will happen under two possible legal rules:

- **Polluters are not liable.** In that case, Elliot will pay Chloe \$50 to take the steps to avoid \$100 worth of uncompensated damage to his property. Elliot pays Chloe because of the economic incentive (it is cheaper to pay Chloe than to repair the damage), not because the law requires him to do so. Total cost to the economy: \$50.
- **Polluters are liable.** In that case, Chloe will spend \$50 on precautions in order to avoid paying Elliot \$100 for the damage she would otherwise cause. In this case, she is motivated by the combination of the legal rules (she is liable) and economic incentives (she would rather pay \$50 than \$100). Total cost to the economy: \$50.

Either way, someone will spend \$50 to avoid spending \$100. The expected value (or cost) to the economy is the same under both rules, so they are equally efficient.

You should notice two things about the Coase Theorem. First, it may appear to have little relevance in the real world because *there are always transaction costs*! There are negotiation costs and litigation costs and costs derived from the uncertainty of whether the harm will occur or how much it is really worth. Nevertheless, the Coase Theorem is a useful starting place because it allows you to see transaction costs as distinct from other types of costs. You may not reach perfect economic efficiency, but you may be able to tell that some rules are more efficient than others.

Second, neither principles of economic efficiency nor the Coase Theorem tell us anything about the appropriate *allocation* of costs. Look again at the consequences of the two opposite legal rules. In each case, someone will spend $50 to avoid $100 in damage, an efficient result. But in a regime of no liability, Elliot will spend the $50, and in the regime of liability, Chloe will spend it. The Coase Theorem has nothing to say about this choice; ultimately, it is not a purely economic judgment. In other words, economics might be able to tell you what is efficient, but efficiency is only one of many conceivable goals for a legal regime.

Ex ante/Ex post. If you want to analyze the incentives created by a particular legal rule, you also have to think about the differences between ex ante and ex post analysis. Ex ante (meaning "from before") refers to an analysis based on circumstances as they existed before a dispute arose. Ex post (meaning "from afterwards") refers to an analysis that includes the circumstances of the actual dispute. A remedy that returns an injured person to the position she was in prior to the defendant's actions is an ex ante remedy because it returns the plaintiff to the status quo before the violation. Tort remedies, for example, are usually ex ante because they seek to put the injured person back in the position she was in before the tort, as much as possible. Contract remedies can be either ex ante or ex post. A contract remedy that returns the injured party back to the position she was in prior to the breach of contract is ex ante; a remedy that puts her in the position she would have been in if the contract had been performed is an ex post remedy. The difference between ex post and ex ante can also be relevant in thinking about how government regulation should be structured to affect the incentives of those governed by the regulation. Do we want to encourage businesses, for example, to *take* certain actions (in which case we should regulate ex ante, requiring or prohibiting the actions) or to *internalize the costs* of their actions (in which case we can regulate ex post, making them pay for the damage their actions cause)?

Principal-Agent Relationships. One final concept rounds out our discussion of law and economics. Structuring incentives to produce specific behaviors is especially complex when a rule has to govern relationships among people who may start out with different incentives. In a complex world, people often have to rely upon others to act on their behalf. Congress delegates to administrative agencies the responsibility for carrying out statutory goals. The Supreme Court announces doctrine that is effectuated by lower courts. A corporation's board of directors delegates to corporate officers the responsibility of acting on behalf of the corporation. A store owner hires salespeople to sell merchandise. Economics (as well as political science) describes these arrangements as principal-agent relationships: the principal assigns limited powers to the agent in order to increase efficiency. This is a rational move because it allows the principal to obtain a desired benefit at a lower cost—counting both time and money—than doing the work herself.

The problem for Congress, the Supreme Court, the corporate board of directors, and the store owner, however, is that their agents may have conflicting interests. Bureaucrats' policy goals may be at odds with congressional goals, district judges may disagree with a Supreme Court precedent, a company's president may be more concerned about her short-term earnings than the corporation's long-term success, and salespeople may prefer loafing to selling. The principal cannot perfectly control the agent's behavior, but can minimize conflicts through clear directives, regular monitoring, and well-placed incentives. When you are interpreting a statutory grant of authority to an agency, an appellate decision setting forth a doctrine, a corporate charter, or an employment contract, you should consider whether the drafter intended to address these principal-agent concerns. If you are arguing, for example, that a statute allows you to challenge an administrative agency's decision, you may be able to argue that Congress intended to give private parties the power to sound an alarm when the agency acted beyond its authority. Or, if you represent a salesperson denied a promised sales commission, you could argue that the commissions were not an unenforceable gift, as contended by the owner, but rather an incentive designed to align the salesperson's interests with the owner's (both benefit from more sales).

Behavioral Law and Economics

Much of the logical power of law and economics—and therefore of the concepts just discussed—depends on an assumption that people will act rationally. A rational actor takes steps that are most likely to help her achieve her goals and will not be distracted by extraneous or irrelevant information. If people do not act rationally, then legal doctrines based on an assumption of rationality obviously won't achieve their objectives (or at least won't be as effective). So are people rational? Studies suggest that they are not, at least not always or completely. People are subject to well-documented **cognitive biases** that produce *systematic* departures from rational judgment. Here we discuss the most common cognitive biases that might interfere with perfect rationality. We should note that many of these biases stem from **heuristics**—mental shortcuts that allow people to make certain judgments more quickly or easily. When these shortcuts undermine sound decision-making, we call them biases.

Anchoring. When asked to make a numerical estimate, people are affected by the initial number provided. Their estimates, in other words, will be "anchored" by the initial number. Anchoring can be rational when the initial number is informative. The list price of a home, for instance, will have a dramatic effect on offers. Usually, this makes sense because the list price is typically related to the value of the home. But the anchoring effect occurs even when the anchor bears no relation to the value of the item being estimated. For example, experimental jurors who learn that the statutory cap for damages is $500,000 will award significantly more money than jurors in a control group who do not know the statutory cap. This is irrational because the statutory cap has nothing to do with the actual damages in a specific case. This irrationality can complicate our attempts to structure economic incentives.

Endowment Effect. People value goods they own more than goods they do not own. They endow what they have with a higher value, which is called the endowment effect. For example, a person might be willing to pay $5 for a nondescript coffee mug, but if you give it to her, she might be unwilling to sell it for less than $7. Since the same effect applies to things like clean air, this might affect the negotiations between polluters and their neighbors: if the pollution is already occurring, the polluter might value it more highly (and the neighbors might value clean air less highly) than if the polluter wants to move into the neighborhood. It also means that the status quo plays a large role in determining how much people value various things. The importance of the status quo in turn brings to the forefront the allocation problems that law and economics ignores.

Framing Effect. People's choices are influenced by how they categorize or "frame" the options. People will be more likely to take a risk to avoid a loss than to make a gain (even when the risky option and the non-risky option are rationally identical). Such framing effects are common in settlement negotiations. In deciding whether to settle a claim, the plaintiff is choosing whether to accept a certain gain from settlement or to gamble on litigation—which may result in being awarded substantially more than the settlement offer, substantially less than the settlement offer, or nothing at all. The defendant, on the other hand, is choosing whether to accept a certain loss or to gamble on litigation—which may result in a substantially greater loss, a substantially smaller loss, or maybe no loss at all. In such a setting, plaintiffs may be irrationally risk-averse while defendants may be equally irrationally risk-seeking. (A risk-*neutral* person is indifferent between options with unequal risks but equal expected values: such a person considers as equivalent an action with a 10 percent probability of netting $10,000 and an action with an 80 percent probability of netting $1250. Although the former is riskier, the expected value of each is $1,000.) Thus, we cannot assume that comparing the expected values of various courses of actions will necessarily cause all people to make the same choices.

Hindsight Bias. The expression "hindsight is 20/20" assumes that people always view the past clearly. In reality, people overestimate the predictability of past events due to hindsight bias. The law frequently requires that individuals assess whether an event should have been foreseen. Judges and juries, for example, evaluate the foreseeability of events *after* they have occurred. Hindsight bias undermines their ability to do so accurately. So, for example, when juries consider how foreseeable an accident was as part of determining whether a defendant acted reasonably, they will be influenced by the fact that the accident *did* in fact occur—even if that occurrence was very unlikely. In other words, even if the appropriate perspective is ex ante, people may not be able to prevent an ex post perspective from creeping into their analysis.

Self-Serving or Egocentric Bias. People tend to demonstrate a self-serving or egocentric bias by believing things that are consistent with their own interests and overestimating their own abilities. For instance, most law students are sure that they will be in the top 10 percent of their law school classes (by definition, 90 percent of law students won't be!). Plaintiffs and defendants (and their lawyers) often *both* believe that they have the stronger case. People believe that they are careful, even when they are negligent. They believe that they are too smart to be caught if they commit a crime. In short, rationality goes out the window when people are evaluating a decision in which they have a stake. In evaluating economic efficiency or calculating the expected value of an action, then, people will predictably use the wrong monetary values.

Test Your Understanding

Danny slipped and fell on a wet floor in his local grocery store. He hears on the news about a slip-and-fall case in which the plaintiff received a multimillion-dollar award. Danny hires Sasha, an attorney, and tells Sasha that he believes his claim is worth at least $1 million. Sasha's prior experience tells her that Danny's claim is more likely worth less than $25,000.

1. What type of decision-making error is Danny committing?
2. How can Sasha help Danny to correct this error in decision-making?

OTHER USEFUL CONCEPTS

Some important ideas cannot be attributed to a single field or limited to a specific theory. These concepts are nevertheless important to the study and application of law. We gather those here.

Baselines. Some concepts are useful in both economic and non-economic analyses. If you are considering the benefits (monetary and otherwise) of a particular legal rule, you always have to ask, "compared to what?" In an important sense, this question is asking about the baseline against which you are measuring legal rules. Imagine that a group of 25 people has 10 items of equal value, and each person would like to own one. Should they adopt a rule that gives the items to the first 10 people who roll a 4 or higher on a die, and then have the legal system protect their right to own the items? Well, if the alternative (or baseline) is a free-for-all, with everybody constantly trying to steal an item from whomever currently has it, our proposed random-selection-then-legal-protection rule looks pretty good. But if the baseline is that people first earn the item, or that the items rotate, our proposed rule looks very unfair. The choice of baselines can have a huge influence on the evaluation of any proposed rule—and choosing a baseline can be difficult and controversial.

Default Rules. Some legal rules (in the broad sense) are mandatory: individuals cannot agree to disregard them or choose different rules. If the law of contracts in a particular jurisdiction requires that certain types of contracts be in writing, for example, parties can reach an agreement without putting it in writing, but a court will not enforce that agreement. Other rules—including most rules on interpreting contracts—are default rules: they apply only if the parties fail to specify some other rule. Default rules thus operate like the default settings in a word processing program. They are set automatically but can be changed by the user. If you are drafting a document, you must know both the mandatory rules and the default rules in order to understand how a court will interpret those documents. But you must also be able to identify which rules *are* default rules so that you can contract around them if the parties wish to do so.

Slippery Slopes. A common legal argument is to suggest that a criticized legal ruling will ultimately lead to another legal outcome that (almost) everyone agrees is bad. This is often called a slippery slope argument: making the first ruling will start us down the slippery slope to the unpopular outcome. You have certainly heard slippery slope arguments: Constitutional protection for gay marriage will lead to constitutional protection of polygamy; a constitutional right to own a hunting rifle will lead to a constitutional right to own an Uzi submachine gun; giving a zoning exception to a commercial daycare center in a residential neighborhood will lead to zoning exceptions for stores and bars. Slippery slope arguments are valid only to the extent that there is a reason to think that the first ruling (the top of the slope) actually *does* make the later outcome more likely (the bottom of the slope). Perhaps it is difficult to distinguish between the two outcomes; perhaps the original ruling causes problems *because* it is partway down the slope, an unstable place to be, and you fear that those problems will be easier to solve by continuing on the path already set rather than climbing back up to the original position at the top of the slope; or perhaps experience with the first ruling will lead to greater acceptance of what were previously unacceptable outcomes. You should be able to make slippery slope arguments, but you should also be able to argue against them by pointing out how the unpopular bottom-of-the-slope result is actually distinguishable from the top-of-the-slope question of the moment.

Normative/Positive. Another useful concept in evaluating legal rules is the distinction between normative claims and positive claims. A normative claim is a claim about the way things "ought" to be (a prescription), and a positive claim is a statement of the way things "are" (a description). Both normative and positive statements can sometimes be self-evident, without need for further argument: murder is wrong (normative), and this sentence has a colon in it (positive). (Note that a positive statement need not be *true*: "this sentence ends in a question mark" is also a positive statement, but a false one.) But most often, both normative and positive legal claims require additional support and are often intertwined or disguised as one another.

WHAT IF A CONCEPT ISN'T LISTED HERE?

We obviously cannot list all the legal tests and concepts in this introductory review. So, what should you do when you come across a test, concept, or other tool that is not described here?

- **Analogize.** Draw analogies to concepts with which you *are* familiar. Does a new test look more like a rule or a standard? Does it categorize or balance? Is it subjective or objective?
- **Contextualize.** Just as you can sometimes glean the meaning of an unfamiliar word from its context, you can sometimes understand a new legal concept from how and when it is used. For example, if you read a case that gives "*Chevron* deference" to an agency regulation (issued pursuant to a statutory grant of authority) because the court concludes that the agency's interpretation of the statute is reasonable, you can figure out that (1) "*Chevron* deference" is a standard of review; (2) it is a standard, not a rule; and (3) that standard is probably somewhere around "clearly erroneous"—the specifics of the court's reasoning might give you a better idea of exactly how deferential the standard is.
- **Research.** Ask your classmates or consult a study aid or legal dictionary. If you know the source of the concept—economic theory, jurisprudence, or psychology, for example—you might be able to find a resource specific to that discipline. Even searching on the Internet for a term might help you begin to understand it, but be careful about the trustworthiness of any online source. Finally, you can ask the professor during office hours.
- **Teach yourself.** In short, learning new tests, concepts, and tools is just like learning the law generally. Your first year gives you a basic vocabulary, but it is mostly designed to enable you to teach yourself. The ability to teach yourself is truly an indispensable lawyering tool.

Chapter 6

HOW TO LOOK AND BE SMARTER IN THE CLASSROOM AND BEYOND

The aim of this book is to prepare you for law school. The chapters lay out the crucial ideas that you must understand in order to succeed as a law student and lawyer. If you read this book, we believe that you will be well on your way to a great first year in law school. But we expect that as you move forward, you will benefit from some additional resources that allow you to gain a deeper and broader understanding of the law that you are learning. In particular, you may want to put law in historical or jurisprudential context.

Your professors may make offhand references to historical eras and events or to jurisprudential schools of thought. Understanding these allusions will help you understand what they are trying to teach you about the law. And you can also use historical or jurisprudential context to draw deeper connections among cases or gain insights into how and why certain cases were decided. You can keep these insights to yourself, or you can bring them up in class and look even smarter!

This chapter is essentially a "cheat sheet" because it offers an abbreviated review of American history and basic legal theories, which will be useful as you prepare for and participate in class. But, like any other cheat sheet, it merely supplements your learning. We start with history and then move on to the theoretical frameworks. You may know a lot of this material already, or it may be entirely new to you. Either way, pick and choose the pieces that you need.

AN AMERICAN HISTORY REFRESHER

Law is dynamic. It is simultaneously the product of its time and a force in its time. Therefore, you need an appreciation of epochs and events that may have influenced the judicial decisions, legislative enactments, or agency rules that you study. Law students have widely varied training in history. The chronological outline of the first two centuries of American history that follows gives you essential information that is of special salience to the study of American law. If you have an extensive knowledge of American history, this section offers a quick refresher of what you already know with an emphasis on events that are most relevant to your upcoming law school career. If your knowledge of American history is rusty, then this discussion should provide you with key information and serve as a basis for doing more research on events of interest. Either way, it's important to remember that American law cannot be separated from American history and that seemingly nonlegal events are often relevant to legal ones. There are at least four salient reasons to review American history: to interpret American law, to understand the nature and reasons for the disputes you'll study, to recognize the evolution of law, and to predict the next stages in the development of law.

The Early Republic (1776–1820)

The United States is a young country. American colonists declared independence from the British Empire in 1776. The next year, a colonist-elected legislature enacted the nation's first national constitution, the Articles of Confederation. When the Revolutionary War officially ended in 1783, the Articles of Confederation served as the basis for the new republic's government. But by the late 1780s, the Articles (which granted very little authority to the national government) were proving insufficient to govern the newly independent

United States. The war had left the nation in debt, and the Articles left the national government with no way to raise money to repay it. The weakness of the central government also led to difficult foreign relations; with no power over interstate or foreign commerce, Congress could not control how individual states dealt with foreign trade or foreign residents. The individual states, moreover, argued over territory, and imposed tariffs and navigation fees on other states. All these problems, foreign and domestic, led to a nationwide recession in 1785–1786, which served as the final impetus for change.

The response was to call a national convention of state delegates, who met in Philadelphia in the summer of 1787. Over the course of four months, the convention wrote a new constitution from scratch. Compared to the Articles of Confederation, it created a much more powerful national government and imposed various limits on the states. For this reason, among others, it was highly controversial. The supporters of ratification and a strong national government were called "Federalists." James Madison, Alexander Hamilton, and John Jay anonymously published the *Federalist Papers*, a series of articles arguing in favor of ratification. Even today, the *Federalist Papers* inform our understanding of the Constitution. Ratification opponents—called "Anti-Federalists"—were suspicious of this new, more powerful federal government.

The Constitution was successfully ratified in 1788, and the national government began to operate in 1789. George Washington was elected as the first president that year and served two terms before voluntarily declining to seek a third term. Following his example, no president chose to run for a third term until Franklin D. Roosevelt in 1940. The first Congress also convened in 1789 and established the framework of the federal government, including, most importantly for our purposes, the Judiciary Act of 1789, which created the first federal court system. The same year, Congress also proposed the Bill of Rights—the first ten amendments to the Constitution—which was ratified in 1791.

The disputes that had marked the ratification period continued to simmer: the Federalists and Anti-Federalists had different views of the appropriate role of the federal government. In Washington's administration, Alexander Hamilton (as secretary of the treasury) and Thomas Jefferson (who, as secretary of state, favored

Anti-Federalist policies) feuded bitterly as each tried to persuade the president to adopt his views. John Adams, a staunch Federalist who was Washington's vice president and successor, defeated Jefferson in 1796, emboldening the Federalist-controlled Congress to enact laws expanding federal power and limiting dissent. The two parties grew more antagonistic, fighting over both foreign and domestic policy.

In the election of 1800, the Jeffersonians—by then called Republicans (no relation to our current Republican Party)—prevailed in both the presidential and congressional elections. They called for greatly diminished federal power and greater state sovereignty. As president, however, Jefferson used his power almost as broadly as his Federalist predecessors.

During Jefferson's presidency, the Federalists continued to have some influence, especially in the judiciary. Just before Jefferson took office, Adams nominated John Marshall (a moderate Federalist) as Chief Justice, and the lame-duck Federalist Congress confirmed him. Marshall remained Chief Justice for the next 34 years and was a thorn in the side of Republican presidents for most of that time.

Between 1801 and 1825, two significant new controversies developed. First was a growing problem with Europe. The United States struggled to remain neutral in the Napoleonic War between Britain and France, but the war affected both sea routes and trade. In 1812, Congress declared war on Britain over America's claim to neutral shipping rights. Perhaps the best that can be said about the War of 1812 is that the United States survived it. It did, however, have significant domestic effects. The Federalist Party collapsed following its opposition to the war. The various trade problems during the war hastened industrialization in the United States by protecting new businesses from foreign competition and depressing the price of southern cotton (which was denied an overseas market during the war) for northern textile mills. The country's growing workforce contributed to industrializing the economy as well: the first official census in 1790 counted more than 4 million Americans. And wave after wave of immigrants were arriving in the new nation, settling primarily in northern cities.

A second issue was not so easily resolved: the intensifying debate over slavery. The first slave ship arrived in Jamestown, Virginia in 1619. By the time of the Revolution, there were almost 700,000 enslaved blacks in the United States. Public attacks on the institution of slavery began as early as the 1750s, and some northern states began abolishing it after the Revolution. Nevertheless, the Constitution protected both slavery and the slave trade in various ways, although it never referred directly to either. The new Congress did so as well, enacting the Fugitive Slave Act in 1793, which made it a criminal act to assist escaping slaves. In 1808, Congress outlawed the foreign slave trade, but not slavery. Abolitionist sentiment continued to grow, however.

The next few decades were marked by increasing controversy punctuated by short-lived compromises. In 1820, the Missouri Compromise admitted Missouri as a slave state and Maine as a free state, and otherwise prohibited slavery in the territory of the Louisiana Purchase north of the 36°30″ parallel (approximately the southern border of Missouri). Although it held the nation together for a while, the Missouri Compromise deepened sectional antipathies and ultimately failed to resolve the issue.

International Neutrality and Domestic Conflict (1821–1860)

By the second quarter of the nineteenth century, American states were sharply divided into three regional blocs—North, West, and South—defined technically by geography but more meaningfully by their economies and social cultures. Industry, including textile mills and manufacturing plants, became the backbone of the northern economy. The southern economy was centered on agriculture, particularly labor-intensive crops like cotton and tobacco. Many Americans—asserting their "manifest destiny" of ownership of the American continent—spread westward, coming into conflict with Europeans and Native Americans. Combined with the escalating battles over slavery, these economic and social differences contributed to the growing regional divisiveness.

Sectional conflict erupted into violence in the mid-1850s. At that time, the Nebraska Territory was on the brink of statehood. Because it was north of the 36°30″ parallel, it should have been admitted as free under the Missouri Compromise—an outcome opposed by southern leaders. Congress responded with the 1854 Kansas-Nebraska Act, which divided the Nebraska Territory into two states (Kansas and Nebraska) where settlers of each would be allowed to decide on the state's status as slave or free. Northern abolitionists financed settlers in Kansas in an attempt to keep it free. Pro-slavery Missourians responded by flooding into Kansas. The resulting bloodshed put a permanent end to any hope of compromise on slavery. The Civil War had unofficially begun.

The Civil War (1861–1865)

The modern Republican Party was founded in 1854 by opponents of the Kansas-Nebraska Act (Jefferson's Republican Party had changed its name to the Democratic Party in the Jackson era and had faced a variety of opposing parties since then). The Republican Party elected its first Speaker of the House in 1856 and its first president—Abraham Lincoln—in 1860. Lincoln ran with a campaign promise of ending the *expansion* of slavery. He was also determined to hold the United States together, despite southern threats of secession. But 11 states did secede—an act Lincoln declared illegal—and on April 12, 1861, Confederate forces fired on Fort Sumter, in Charleston, South Carolina. This was the official beginning of the Civil War.

It was the bloodiest war in American history, killing more than 600,000 American soldiers and sailors—almost 2 percent of the American population. More Americans died in the Civil War than in all the country's other wars combined. It was also the last major war fought on American soil, and it caused massive economic and cultural disruptions, especially in the South. Most of the battles were fought in Confederate territory. The war took its toll on civil liberties in the North as well: Lincoln suspended the writ of habeas corpus (used to challenge the legality of a person's imprisonment) and approved measures that substantially curtailed the rights of dissenters. The "war between the states" ended four years after it began, on April 9, 1865, when Confederate General Robert E. Lee surrendered to Union General Ulysses S. Grant on the courthouse steps in Appomattox, Virginia.

Between the time the Civil War began and the time it ended, a war that had started as an attempt to end the *extension* of slavery and keep the union together became dedicated to *abolishing* slavery. In 1863, President Lincoln issued the Emancipation Proclamation, declaring all enslaved people in Confederate states (but not Union states) free. It was not until 1865, in the closing months of the war, that Congress proposed the Thirteenth Amendment, abolishing slavery. The Amendment was declared ratified in December, after the war had ended.

Lincoln did not live to see the abolition of slavery; he was assassinated on April 14, 1865, five days after Lee's surrender. His controversial vice president, southern Democrat Andrew Johnson, took the oath of office and a new battle began between Congress and the president over how to "reconstruct" the defeated South.

Reconstruction (1865–1877)

In many ways, the Civil War and its aftermath produced a rebirth of the American republic. The Reconstruction period, sometimes called the "Second Founding," saw the enactment of three important constitutional amendments: the Thirteenth, Fourteenth, and Fifteenth Amendments, together called the "Reconstruction Amendments." Congress also enacted foundational civil rights legislation during this period.

The most difficult task facing America after the war was reuniting a divided nation. The Republican Party, which controlled Congress, was divided about how to "reconstruct" the former Confederate states. How harshly should they be treated? How easily should they be readmitted to the Union? And what protections, if any, were needed for newly freed blacks? The South's response to the war did not make the choices easier. Southern states enacted "Black Codes"—civil and criminal statutes that effectively prevented many black citizens from owning or renting land, limited the jobs that they could hold, and set curfews and other restrictions on their freedom of movement. Most astonishingly, these laws attempted to recreate slavery by granting courts broad powers to order, upon minimal pretext, blacks to work as household servants, farm laborers, or apprentices at little or no pay.

The contentious relationship between Congress and President Johnson worsened the situation. While most Republicans wanted the defeated southern states to guarantee good behavior, Johnson was willing to readmit the secessionist states as soon as they ratified the Thirteenth Amendment. He also vetoed several important pieces of legislation designed to undermine the Black Codes and to protect the newly freed slaves (Congress overrode most of these vetoes). In 1868, the House of Representatives voted to impeach—a Congressional declaration of wrongdoing by a public official—Johnson, but the Senate acquitted him by a single vote.

Congress responded on several fronts to the actions of the southern states. In 1866, they sent to the states an amendment—the Fourteenth—which, among other things, granted citizenship to anyone born in the United States and guaranteed all citizens the equal protection of the laws. The former Confederate states almost uniformly rejected it. Congressional Republicans responded by imposing military rule, over Johnson's veto, on former Confederate states. The Military Reconstruction Act gave blacks the right to vote and conditioned readmission to the Union on ratification of the Fourteenth Amendment. While the Fourteenth was ratified in 1868 (and the Fifteenth, providing that the right to vote could not be denied on the basis of race, in 1870), federal troops remained in parts of the South until 1877 when a new president—Republican Rutherford Hayes—took office after a special commission resolved an electoral-vote dispute in his favor.

The Gilded Age (1878–1901)

Without federal enforcement of the Reconstruction Amendments and legislation, southern states quickly moved to disenfranchise blacks and deprive them of other rights. Racial discrimination ranged from moderate to violent. The Ku Klux Klan, founded in 1866, engaged in a continued campaign of terror that included lynchings. Southern legislatures disenfranchised most blacks by imposing poll taxes and political literacy tests, while allowing whites to vote if their grandfathers had done so. The southern states also enacted what became known as "Jim Crow" laws, which denied blacks most other basic rights and enforced public segregation. The U.S. Supreme Court acquiesced in the abandonment of equal rights: in a series of cases between 1882 and 1896, it struck down several Reconstruction-era statutes and interpreted the Fourteenth Amendment to allow legally enforced segregation under the rubric of "separate but equal."

Besides race discrimination, the hallmark of this period was the triumph of virtually unrestricted capitalism, earning the era the name the "Gilded Age." Economic power was consolidated in the hands of a small number of wealthy owners, sometimes derogatorily called "robber barons," who presided over and profited from the enormous economic industrial development that took place after the Civil War. This "era of big business" dates from the creation of the Standard Oil Trust in 1881. A "trust" is a legal entity used to assign control over dispersed assets to someone other than the owner. By consolidating scattered businesses into trusts, the owners of these companies, through trustees, could dominate related industries and prevent competition. Congress enacted the Interstate Commerce Act in 1887 and the Sherman Antitrust Act in 1890, which seemed meant to limit the monopolistic economic power of the big trust companies. But prosecutions were few and far between; cases against defendants that were tried were rarely successful.

As capital accumulated in the hands of a few, public dissatisfaction with economic conditions grew. Labor unions had expanded with industry and demanded—often unsuccessfully—improved labor conditions. Farmers in the South and West also began clamoring for change. When pro-business President William McKinley was assassinated in 1901 (the third president to meet that fate), he was succeeded by a vice president with decidedly different views, Theodore "Teddy" Roosevelt. The age of the Progressives had begun.

The Progressive Era and the Great War (1901–1919)

Teddy Roosevelt assumed leadership as the country entered a new century that brought with it high expectations for change and reform. Progressivism—the name for the reform movement—was not a single movement, but rather disparate strands connected by some common themes. Progressives supported higher wages and better working conditions and opposed corporate robber barons and urban political bosses. They viewed all these goals as intertwined: better government would act to cure social ills and protect the citizenry through regulation of business. In this way, America would "progress." But Progressives also supported the eugenics movement, arguing that America would make progress by sterilizing citizens with "undesirable" attributes. They largely ignored race discrimination, sharing the racial prejudice of most white Americans of the time.

During Teddy Roosevelt's presidency, some Progressive ideas were implemented. At his urging, Congress created a Department of Commerce and Labor. His Justice Department sued some of the largest trusts. He persuaded Congress to regulate (or increase the regulation of) various industries, including the railroads, food producers, and the meat-packing industry.

Despite Roosevelt's Progressive accomplishments, America's first truly Progressive president was Democrat Woodrow Wilson, who took office in 1913. During his presidency, the country ratified the Sixteenth Amendment, which allowed Congress to enact a progressive income tax. He convinced Congress to establish the Federal Trade Commission and enact the Clayton Antitrust Act to combat the still-powerful monopolistic trusts. Domestic issues were quickly overshadowed by foreign policy issues, however.

The Great War—now known as World War I—began in Europe in 1914. America quickly declared its neutrality. But by Wilson's second term, German submarine attacks on American ships in the north Atlantic, as well as other factors, propelled the United States in 1917 to declare war on Germany and join the Allied forces of Great Britain and France. Repeating the pattern of earlier wars and other crises, the federal government dramatically restricted civil liberties and clamped down on dissent during the war. America's involvement in World War I was relatively brief. The Allied forces reached an armistice with Germany in November 1918, and the Treaty of Versailles was signed the following June, officially ending the war.

The Roaring Twenties (1920–1929)

The end of World War I ushered in a period of tremendous prosperity fueled by economic mobilization to support the war (which turned to domestic manufacturing after the war), government policies favoring businesses after the war, an explosion in automobile and air transportation, and a general feeling of optimism. The Constitution also saw change, with the adoption of the Nineteenth Amendment, granting women the right to vote.

The end of the war also brought isolationism and xenophobia. Congress imposed a series of quotas on immigration from various countries, mostly southern and eastern European countries. In 1924, they prohibited all Asian immigration. Other "outsiders," including dissenters, were also left out of the action. As the Bolshevik revolution in Russia succeeded and Josef Stalin consolidated his power, the United States experienced its first "Red Scare," beginning under Wilson and continuing into the 1920s. The U.S. attorney general carried out extensive investigations of suspected Communists and Communist sympathizers. Arrests, imprisonments, and deportations occurred on little or no evidence.

The new economic prosperity did not benefit everyone. Farm debt mounted, and fledgling labor unions had little success against big business. Rising prices, meanwhile, made it hard for the poor—whether rural or urban—to buy necessities. Even for those who benefited from the new prosperity, the economic policies of the age had a downside. Much of the economic growth was fueled by speculators who bought stock "on margin" (with no money paid up front). The government did nothing to stop such speculation. These maneuvers worked only while the stock market continued to rise—and it could not do so indefinitely. In October 1929, the stock market crashed, marking the start of an economic depression that would last for more than a decade.

The Depression and the New Deal (1929–1941)

During the first four weeks of October 1929, the New York Stock Exchange lost 37 percent of its value. It finally collapsed entirely on October 29, 1929, "Black Tuesday," ushering in the Great Depression—the worst economic period in the history of the United States. Between 1929 and 1932, personal income in the country fell by half; one in four Americans was out of work; over 9,000 banks failed or closed; and thousands of other businesses, from factories to farms, went out of business. By 1933, over 13 million people were unemployed, and millions more were underemployed. A million people lived in shanty towns called "Hoovervilles," after President Herbert Hoover. President Hoover and Congress refused to provide any government aid to the impoverished masses, believing that private charity was preferable to a government "dole."

With America at the breaking point, Democratic presidential nominee Franklin Delano Roosevelt (FDR) handily defeated Hoover in the 1932 election. The new president moved quickly after his March 1933 inauguration to implement his "New Deal." In what remains the most productive first 100 days of any administration, FDR (with the support of large Democratic majorities in Congress) passed 15 *major* proposals, including measures setting standards for businesses, banks, and securities to build confidence in American markets and to decrease the risk and extent of economic crises. The laws passed by the 73rd Congress (1933–1935) include many that define modern American government, including the law creating the Federal Deposit Insurance Corporation, the Fair Labor Standards Act, the National Labor Relations Act, the Securities Exchange Act, and the Social Security Act. Congress also established numerous administrative agencies, permanently changing the shape of American government, and hired millions of Americans in public works projects under the Works Progress Administration (WPA).

During his first term, President Roosevelt appeared almost unstoppable. His one major challenge proved to be the Supreme Court, which was controlled by five Republicans, including four staunch economic conservatives nicknamed the "Four Horsemen of the Apocalypse"—Justices George Sutherland, Pierce Butler, James McReynolds, and Willis Van Devanter. Beginning in 1935, the Court struck down several key parts of the New Deal program as unconstitutional. Not a single vacancy occurred during FDR's first term, so the Court remained unchanged.

Following his landslide reelection in 1936, FDR proposed a plan to allow him to appoint up to six additional Justices—one for each Justice over age 70—to the Supreme Court. The Constitution does not set the number of Justices, and Congress had changed the number six times since 1789. The public and many Democratic leaders were nevertheless outraged by FDR's proposal, which was quickly dubbed the "Court-packing plan." This proved to be FDR's first significant setback in popular opinion and political support, contributing to a loss in his momentum. While Congress debated the Court-packing plan, it became moot: in 1937, the Court voted to uphold two key New Deal statutes. The change was due to Justice Owen Roberts; although he had often voted with the Four Horsemen, he voted with the liberal Justices in these two cases. His complex motivations have been the subject of much historical analysis, but his apparent change of sides has been called "the switch in time that saved nine." Justice Van Devanter shortly thereafter announced his retirement. The Senate quickly confirmed FDR's nominee, Alabama Senator Hugo Black, to fill the empty seat. By 1940, FDR had appointed a majority of the Justices. He eventually would fill every seat save one. Only President Washington named more Justices.

World War II (1941–1945)

While economic woes dominated U.S. domestic concerns, tensions were growing in Europe. In 1939, Nazi Germany, led by Adolph Hitler, invaded Poland, sparking the Second World War. Allied with Italy, Germany pursued a plan of European domination. While not formally joining the war, the United States began to prepare for war. Foreign affairs energized FDR, who was near the end of a difficult second term and frustrated by continued economic woes and political battles. He opted to seek a record third term and won on the slogan "don't switch horses in the middle of the stream."

As the situation in Europe deteriorated, Congress agreed to sell arms and equipment to the European allies fighting Hitler. This was the final boost the economy needed: war production put millions of factories back into production and millions of Americans back to work. By the fall of 1941, although the United States was still officially neutral, it was clear that the country was headed for war.

Meanwhile, in Asia, a military dictatorship had taken control of Japan and began attacking other Asian nations. In September 1940, Japan and Germany entered a formal military alliance. Japanese bombers attacked America's primary Pacific military base, Pearl Harbor in Hawaii, on December 7, 1941, which Roosevelt called a "date which will live in infamy." Almost 3,000 U.S. soldiers, sailors, and civilians died in Pearl Harbor, and much of the U.S. fleet in the Pacific was destroyed. Congress declared war on Japan on December 8. Three days later, Germany and Italy declared war on the United States, and the United States declared war on them in return.

The war in Europe, though horrific, had few major domestic repercussions beyond those of wartime generally. Not so in the Pacific. There were fears that Japan, having bombed Hawaii, might be able to attack the continental United States. These fears were almost certainly unreasonable, but they were fanned by another factor: racism. Anti-Asian sentiment had grown during the first half of the twentieth century. The economic success of Japanese Americans in California caused further resentment.

In 1942, a series of executive orders by President Roosevelt and a statute enacted by Congress first imposed a curfew on Japanese Americans living on the West Coast, and then forced them to relocate to internment camps elsewhere in the United States. Almost all of them were citizens, many had never even been to Japan, and not one was ever proved disloyal. Indeed, many Japanese Americans fought in the U.S. military against Japan and Germany. Nonetheless, they lost their homes, their businesses, and their livelihoods (many of which were snapped up by their white neighbors), along with their freedom, when they were forcibly relocated. The Supreme Court upheld the program over strong dissents by Justices Frank Murphy and Robert Jackson. Both the program and the Supreme Court decision were based in part on false information provided by the military—although the executive and judicial branches seemed all too willing to believe the falsehoods. In 1988, Congress passed a law apologizing for the internment program and providing reparations.

The European war finally ended when Germany surrendered on May 7, 1945. President Roosevelt, elected to office four times, did not live to see the end of the war; he collapsed and died on April 12. He was succeeded by Vice President Harry S. Truman, who had been in office only four months (he had not been Roosevelt's running mate in earlier elections). After the victory in Europe, Truman turned his attention to Japan, which had not yet surrendered.

In August 1945, Truman authorized what would become perhaps the most far-reaching event of the war. On August 6, America dropped the first atomic bomb on Hiroshima, Japan. Almost 100,000 Japanese (military and civilian) were killed instantly and an equal number grievously wounded, many of whom would later die of their wounds or of radiation poisoning. Japan did not surrender. Three days later, a second bomb was dropped on Nagasaki, with similar devastation. Japan surrendered. World War II was over, but the nuclear age had just begun.

The Cold War (1945–1990)

Two world powers emerged from the war: the United States and the Soviet Union (or USSR). As the Soviet Union marched toward Berlin at the end of World War II, it brought Communism to the countries that it had liberated from Nazi Germany, drawing an "iron curtain" between eastern and western Europe. In response, the United States adopted a series of policies aimed at containing the Soviet Union's influence, including the creation of the North Atlantic Treaty Organization (NATO), the Truman Doctrine guaranteeing U.S. assistance in preventing the spread of Communism, and, at times, a commitment to the "domino theory" that if one country became Communist, others in the region would also fall. The USSR countered with the Warsaw Pact, an alliance among the USSR and its satellite "Eastern Bloc" countries, and its own efforts to protect countries that adopted Communist doctrine. The United States and USSR were in a standoff that became known as the Cold War.

The key to understanding the Cold War is to recognize that the United States and the USSR never fought each other directly: it was a war of proxies. This proxy war was fought on several fronts: the Greek civil war shortly after World War II, the Korean War in the early 1950s, the building of the Berlin Wall in 1961, the Cuban Missile Crisis in 1962, and the Vietnam War from the 1960s into the 1970s. While the Cuban Missile Crisis came closest to U.S. soil and nearly resulted in nuclear war, the Vietnam War may have had the most far-reaching effects on political, social, and legal developments at home. As we discuss in the next two sections, it affected the shape and direction of the civil rights movement and the policies of three presidents. The war in Vietnam was a catalyst for domestic strife. It continued for more than ten years, ultimately killing 50,000 Americans (as well as many more Vietnamese) and changing American culture.

The Cold War had three other domestic effects. First was the massive military expenditures necessitated by the arms race and the war in Vietnam. A second, also expensive result was the space race, starting with the Soviet Union's successful launch of the first unmanned satellite in 1957 and culminating in Neil Armstrong's first steps on the moon in 1969. Finally, the Cold War and the accompanying fear of Communism led to a second Red Scare in the 1950s. No one was immune from the hunt for Communist infiltrators. The House Un-American Activities Committee (HUAC) investigated anyone—in and out of the government—who was suspected of leaning left. HUAC grilled individuals in public hearings, demanding that they implicate friends and associates. Freedom of speech and association were trampled as Congress passed laws penalizing members of the American Communist Party.

While the repressive program was broad-based, it came to be symbolized by one man: Senator Joseph McCarthy, a Republican senator from Wisconsin. He claimed to have lists of hundreds of Communists in the State Department and other government entities. His "Communist witch hunts" destroyed the lives and reputations of many loyal Americans. The pervasive search for "Communists under the bed" came to be known as McCarthyism, and it lasted through much of the 1950s. McCarthy eventually lost his credibility and the most serious civil rights violations ceased, but the fear of Communism persisted until the end of the Cold War.

The Cold War finally wound to a close in the early 1990s. The Soviet Union gradually relaxed its social and economic policies, including its grip on Warsaw Pact nations, and by 1989, all Soviet satellite countries had overthrown their Communist leaders. The most dramatic events took place in Germany, where demonstrators tore down the Berlin wall. Just as the building of the wall had served as a tangible symbol of the Cold War, its destruction represented the end of that war. Germany reunited in 1990, and shortly afterward the Soviet Union cracked apart. The Cold War was over.

The Civil Rights Movement (1954–1972)

The civil rights movement is often dated to the landmark 1954 Supreme Court decision in *Brown v. Board of Education* holding that separate schools are inherently unequal and therefore unconstitutional. But that decision was actually the product of a litigation strategy that dates to Thurgood Marshall and Charles Houston's founding of the NAACP Legal Defense Fund (LDF) in 1940. The first nongovernmental organization created for the sole purpose of public interest litigation, the NAACP LDF originated the "test-case" strategy. Rather than attacking the separate-but-equal doctrine directly, the LDF chipped away at the doctrine through a series of cases raising narrow legal questions and creating a set of favorable decisions upon which to build. Eventually, these individual cases led to *Brown*.

Protests were another crucial part of the civil rights movement. In the South, life was still largely segregated in the 1950s and early 1960s. Peaceful, organized protests—from bus boycotts to public marches—drew national and international attention and support. The often violent responses of police, elected officials, and whites exposed the southern resistance to equal rights and integration. Martin Luther King, Jr., an influential young leader of the bus boycott movement, helped found the Southern Christian Leadership Conference, which carried out a campaign of nonviolent resistance to segregation and discrimination.

After *Brown*, the Supreme Court and lower federal courts continued to order the desegregation of other public facilities. In 1967, the Court invalidated laws against interracial marriage. Throughout the 1950s and 1960s, the Court also revolutionized the American criminal justice system, largely in response to its failure to deliver equal justice. Perhaps the best-known example is *Gideon v. Wainwright* (1963), which held that state and federal governments had to provide lawyers to indigent defendants.

Congress passed a series of civil rights laws, including two Voting Rights Acts and the Civil Rights Act of 1964. The latter was a comprehensive antidiscrimination statute, prohibiting discrimination in employment, education, and public places. It prohibited not only race discrimination, but also discrimination on the basis of religion, color, or national origin. The Court and the country continued to make progress against race discrimination of all sorts, and in 1967, Thurgood Marshall became the first African American Supreme Court Justice.

Sex discrimination was as well entrenched in U.S. society as race discrimination. The original version of the Civil Rights Act of 1964 did not address discrimination based on sex. The final law added sex to the equal employment opportunity section ("Title VII") but not to the sections prohibiting discrimination in schools or public places. The National Organization of Women was founded in 1966 to address continued discrimination against women in employment despite the 1964 act and to advocate for the expansion of protection to include discrimination by educational institutions. Even at co-educational institutions, women often lacked access to certain degree programs and to co-curricular activities. In law, for example, one in five law school classes had no women students in 1964. Title IX of the Education Amendments of 1972 wrought tremendous change to the educational experiences of girls and women. Before Title IX, only 10 percent of law students and 5 percent of law professors were women. By 1980, nearly 40 percent of law students and more than 10 percent of law professors were women. Today, over half of law students and close to half of law professors are women. The first female Supreme Court Justice, Sandra Day O'Connor, was nominated and confirmed in 1981; by 2024, four out of nine justices are women.

The Great Society and the Age of Protest (1960–1976)

In 1960, Democrat John Fitzgerald Kennedy (JFK) was elected on an ambitious platform of conquering the "New Frontier" of "unfulfilled hopes and dreams." We will never know whether Kennedy would eventually have achieved those goals. On November 22, 1963, while campaigning for reelection in Dallas, Texas, Kennedy was assassinated. His vice president, Lyndon Baines Johnson, took the oath of office on Air Force One as it carried him and the body of his predecessor back to Washington.

Johnson (or LBJ) was a born politician, a Texan who had served many years in Congress, and he accomplished what Kennedy did not. His "Great Society" program—pushed through Congress largely by the force of his personality—expanded FDR's New Deal to include the Job Corps, the Teacher Corps, Medicare, Medicaid, and many other government programs to fight the "War on Poverty." Some argue that in his first 100 days, LBJ outdid even FDR. He was reelected by a landslide in 1964. His Republican opponent, Barry Goldwater, won only his home state of Arizona and a handful of states in the South, marking the beginning of the southern shift from Democratic (since the Civil War) to Republican.

But Johnson was undone by the escalating war in Vietnam and the increasing protests at home. Opposition to the war grew, and with it, dissatisfaction with the Johnson administration. The second half of the 1960s saw hundreds of thousands of Americans march on Washington in a series of protests, some demanding an end to the war and others demanding equality for African Americans. Despite his early accomplishments, LBJ's second term became defined by the war in Vietnam. He decided not to run for reelection in 1968. That year was perhaps the most difficult of the 1960s, with the assassinations of Martin Luther King, Jr., and Robert F. Kennedy (President Kennedy's younger brother who was seeking the Democratic presidential nomination), race riots in numerous cities, and a Democratic presidential convention in Chicago marked by violent clashes between protestors and police. When the year was over, Republican Richard Nixon (who had been Dwight D. Eisenhower's vice president from 1953 to 1961) had defeated Democrat Hubert H. Humphrey (who had been LBJ's vice president from 1965 to 1969) for the presidency.

Nixon was reelected by a landslide in 1972. But during the presidential campaign, Nixon aides had engineered a burglary at Democratic headquarters at the Watergate hotel and apartment complex in Washington, D.C. When the burglary came to light in 1973, Nixon denied any involvement, but many suspected that he was involved in either the burglary or its cover-up, or both. Nixon appointed a special prosecutor, Archibald Cox, to investigate the burglary. But on October 20, 1973, in the "Saturday Night Massacre," Nixon ordered his attorney general, Elliot Richardson, to fire Cox. Richardson refused and resigned, as did Deputy Attorney General William Ruckelshaus. Cox was finally fired by Solicitor General Robert Bork.

Meanwhile, a federal grand jury indicted a number of Nixon associates for conspiracy to obstruct justice and named Nixon as an unindicted co-conspirator. In the course of that criminal proceeding, a federal court ordered Nixon to turn over tapes of conversations in the Oval Office. Nixon refused, but on July 24, 1974, the Supreme Court ordered him to produce the tapes. He did produce them, including a tape on which he was heard authorizing hush money for one of the burglars. He resigned the presidency—the only president ever to do so—on August 9, to avoid almost certain impeachment and conviction. His successor, Gerald Ford, had himself been appointed (rather than elected) as vice president after Nixon's first vice president, Spiro Agnew, resigned after being charged with having taken bribes. One of Ford's first official acts was to pardon Nixon for any crimes he might have committed.

The year 1976 marked the two-hundredth anniversary of the founding of the United States of America. It was celebrated across the country with great fanfare. The first two centuries saw astonishing achievements and a remarkable pace of change, but also war, violence, and other problems. We have only skimmed across the surface of those two centuries, but it should be enough to get you started thinking about the many ways that events might influence law and vice versa.

THEORETICAL FRAMEWORKS OF AMERICAN LAW

American law is influenced by theories or philosophies of law known as **jurisprudence** (from *juris* meaning "of law" and *prudentia* meaning "knowledge"). In the course of your legal education, you will hear these theories mentioned directly or indirectly, and you also will use them, consciously or not, in your analysis of legal problems. Theories of law ask foundational questions: What is law? What is its purpose? What is its origin and nature? Where does it lead? These questions may appear simple, but in fact they are enormous and complex. We cannot canvass the varied and multilayered theories of law in these next few pages, but we can hope to introduce several prominent theories, offering a brief description of each theory.

Any evaluation of a problem, including how the law should respond to it (and indeed *whether* it should respond at all), is inevitably and unavoidably informed by a person's notions of rights and responsibilities, the role of law and legal institutions, and so on. Just as law from a particular time period is influenced by nonlegal events (why you must know history to understand law), law also necessarily reflects the dominant philosophy of law of that time. Critiques of (or responses to) a legal doctrine or legal institution often reflect one or more contemporary theories of law. If you understand basic jurisprudential approaches, you will better understand the content and evolution of law, and perhaps be better able to predict its future path–something your clients will always want to know. You will also be a more persuasive advocate if you appreciate the underpinnings for your arguments because doing so will allow you to connect different arguments, doctrines, and questions. Finally, a basic familiarity with the core jurisprudential theories–particularly recognizing the hallmarks of each–should allow you to identify some of the arguments made by your professors, your classmates, and even yourself as falling within one of the theories.

These theories are rich and multifaceted. Various schools of thought thrive under each banner. We cannot impart the full subtlety and complexity of the ideas in this brief overview. In order to aid your understanding, we organize our discussion by considering the theories according to their primary focus:

1. the nature of law,
2. the role of judges,

3. the goals of law, and
4. critical perspectives on law.

This organization is highly debatable, but we offer it for the limited purpose of helping you to understand the theories.

The Nature of Law

What is law? Historically, the two most important answers to this question are **natural law theory** and **legal positivism.** Natural law theorists assert that morality or other principles outside law determine the content of the law in some way. Legal positivists deny this and assert instead that the content of our legal rights and obligations is determined by social facts such as the shared recognition of the authority of the Constitution and the power of Congress to enact new laws.

Natural law theory is difficult to present accurately because its critics, including legal positivists, assigned the label "natural law" to a variety of views in order to support their own ideas rather than to offer an accurate portrait of natural law. Natural law is most strongly associated with the legal maxim *lex injusta est non lex*, or "an unjust law is not a (true) law." This phrase expresses the idea that legal validity, obligation, or authority is not independent of the content of the law. Things get confusing because the same phrase "natural law" is also applied to a moral theory—the view that our moral obligations are a function of moral rules that can be discovered by human reasoning. The two different kinds of "natural law" can go together—if the standard for what counts as an unjust (and hence invalid) legal rule is the moral natural law. But natural law theory as a *legal* theory can be built on any principles, including consequentialist views like utilitarianism (see discussion below) or character-centered ones like Aristotle's theory of human excellence or virtue. A paradigmatic natural law argument would be: "That is not a valid law because the content of that law is unjust."

Legal positivism asserts that law is the product of institutions. Legal positivism developed as a reaction to natural law, which legal positivists viewed as nothing more than "private opinion in disguise." Early positivists argued that law was the command of a sovereign—an authority who regularly is obeyed but who does not regularly obey any other authority—backed by the threat of punishment. Later, more sophisticated positivists suggested that valid laws are identified by a complex social rule—the "rule of recognition"—that identifies which institutions have the authority to enact statutes, make common law, and so forth.

Adjudication Theories

Adjudication theories have had a dramatic influence on American legal education. Indeed, classical legal theory (or formalism) and legal realism, contrasting positive theories of law, dominated the study of law for much of the twentieth century. Two more recent approaches, legal process and legal pragmatism, adopt a middle ground between formalism and realism.

Classical legal theory, also referred to as **formalism**, emphasizes the constraining role of legal texts and holds that applying conventional methods of legal reasoning to those texts generally produces a clear answer. Classical formalism manifests itself in modern jurisprudence primarily in theories of constitutional and statutory interpretation: modern formalists generally urge a strict adherence to the literal text as a way to constrain judicial discretion. Formalist theories of statutory interpretation focus on the plain meaning of statutory provisions and dismiss or downplay the role of legislative intent or the purposes of the law in question. The most prominent formalist theory of constitutional interpretation is **originalism**, which, as its name suggests, seeks to reveal and give effect to the original meaning of the Constitution as understood at the time of its enactment.

Legal realism began in the 1930s as a challenge to formalism. Legal realists argued that a judge cannot and should not decide cases without considering the context and consequences of her decision, or without the influence of the judge's own thoughts and experiences. One enduring realist idea concerns the indeterminacy (or, more precisely, "*under*-determinacy") of many appellate cases, which results from the large number of sometimes contradictory legal principles that can be used to interpret statutes and narrow or broaden judicial holdings. Another important realist idea is that many areas of law can be better understood if we turn our attention away from the general language of the statutes or holdings and turn instead to what might be called "situation-types"—fact patterns that recur and elicit consistent patterns of decisions from judges even though the decisions do not seem to be a function of the legal rules themselves. Finally, contemporary legal theory and practice has incorporated the realist insight that in many areas of law (for example, commercial law), courts look to "commercial practice" or relevant social norms to determine what the law requires.

The **legal process** movement arose in the 1950s in reaction to legal realism. Legal process scholars focused on orderly legal procedures rather than on substantive rules. They emphasized the value of "reasoned elaboration" by judges (and other decision-makers) and the relevance of "institutional competence." While formalists expect cases to be governed by legal rules announced in advance and realists deny that they are governable at all, process theorists find a fair hearing before an unbiased, principled tribunal sufficient (and the best that any legal system can provide). Whatever substantive rules those tribunals create and apply will ultimately be adequate. This conclusion is also the theory's greatest flaw: the application of neutral procedures may nevertheless lead to abhorrent substantive outcomes. While there are few contemporary process theorists, process insights live on in the emphasis in many legal doctrines on fair procedures. Moreover, the general aim of the legal process school—the integration of arguments of policy and principle into doctrinal legal scholarship—has been accepted by lawyers, judges, and legal scholars.

Legal pragmatism is the most recent attempt to achieve a balance between the formalist and realist views of the determinacy of law. Legal pragmatists contend that there exists a median between constraint and discretion. This pragmatic midpoint is a function of the legal context of a case or issue, including precedent, history, social norms, politics, and policy. Judicial decisions are thus principled and constrained but not fully determinate.

The Goals of Law

What is the goal or purpose of law and legal institutions? Numerous legal philosophers have grappled with this question and have offered different answers. We focus on three types here: justice theories, utilitarianism, and law and economics.

Justice theories begin with the recognition that laws do not always serve justice. Should they? Justice theories of law believe that they *must* serve justice and are premised on the idea that the *purpose* of law is substantive justice. Of course, there is disagreement about what constitutes substantive justice! All modern debates regarding justice have revolved around John Rawls's *A Theory of Justice* (1972). Rawls, building on the social contract idea, argued for "justice as fairness." Rawls asked what principles of justice would be adopted in a hypothetical "original position" in which the parties choose principles of justice behind a "veil of ignorance"—not knowing what attributes or position they might have in the world. The core idea of Rawls's thought experiment is to ask the question, "What principles of justice would be chosen under conditions that are fair to everyone?" The veil of ignorance is introduced so that arbitrary considerations and interests of the parties do not bias the principles of justice.

Utilitarianism argues that law should facilitate the maximization of collective well-being. Simple utilitarianism defines this as the "greatest happiness of the greatest number." More complex utilitarianism rejects the equation of happiness with pleasure (or the opposite of pain), and argues instead that "higher" pleasures, especially those related to intellectual pursuits, should be treated as more valuable than simpler ones. Utilitarianism is an elegant, egalitarian conception of law's function, but the specifics of the theory are heavily debated.

Law and economics (or **economic analysis of law**) responds to at least some of the unanswered questions of utilitarianism. First, law and economics asserts that happiness (or "utility") is measured through "revealed preferences": people try to obtain what they want, and thus their choices reveal what makes them happy. The *amount* of happiness is measured by what people are is willing to give (typically money) in order to obtain what they want. Second, law can maximize happiness (or utility) by advancing efficiency. Law and economics scholars generally define efficiency as maximizing the amount by which benefits outweigh costs.

Law and economics has been one of the dominant philosophies in law schools since the early 1980s. You should expect economic analysis to be part of many of your classes. (Chapter 5 explains the key concepts from law and economics as well as criticisms of those concepts, including those developed as part of Behavioral Law and Economics.)

Critical Theories

Critical legal theories are called "critical" because they critically assess core assumptions of law, as well as of the legal theories that justify (or rationalize) the law. Critical scholars contend that the law reflects and reinforces the existing political and economic power structure of which judges are a part.

Critical legal studies (CLS), which began in the late 1970s, posits that law and society cannot be separated, and thus, that law inevitably legitimates, privileges, and perpetuates the preexisting hierarchy, ensuring the continued dominance of the wealthy and powerful. Critical legal scholars (or "Crits") contend that legal rules are not inevitable or natural, but are rather the product of particular circumstances and thus variable and ultimately indeterminate. They deconstruct different areas of law as well as different jurisprudential approaches to reveal systematic errors and biases. But because they find everything (not just law) indeterminate, they (generally) do not propose solutions to the numerous shortcomings that they find. Their favorite type of scholarship, by their own admission, is "trashing": tearing down or deconstructing existing legal doctrines without proposing replacements.

Critical race theory (CRT), like critical legal studies, seeks to reveal the biases inherent in existing American law. But, as its name implies, CRT focuses on how law and legal institutions reflect and institutionalize racism. Critical race theorists contend that the American legal system is the product of oppressive, discriminatory, and unequal economic, political, and social forces and ask how such a regime can protect the disadvantaged. Whereas CLS generally fails to propose solutions to identified problems, CRT and feminist legal theory (discussed below) focus a great deal of energy on specific proposals to address the injustices that they identify. In addition to arguing that racism is pervasive in law, critical race theorists also argue that minorities have distinctive experiences that are not recognized in conventional discourse in law schools or the legal system generally. CRT scholarship often uses nontraditional methods—such as first-person narrative and allegory—in order to interject the personal experiences of historically subordinated groups into legal discourse.

Feminist legal theory focuses on the role of gender in the law. Like critical legal studies and critical race theory, feminists argue that the content and structure of law reflects and reinforces biases in society. But where CLS focuses on socioeconomic or political bias and CRT on racial and ethnic bias, feminists focus on gender bias. Three distinct approaches to feminist legal theory are worth mentioning. **Liberal feminists** contend that the state's first role is to protect individual rights and liberty and that women should be treated the same as men in this regard. **Cultural feminists** argue that men and women think, reason, and approach the world in fundamentally different ways and that legal recognition of those differences can be empowering to women, for example, by requiring employers to accommodate women's family obligations. **Radical feminists** maintain that law is simply a reflection of the preferences of the powerful and that objectivity and rationality are myths. They argue that the law itself creates and perpetuates differences between men and women and incorporates sexism and gender-based biases.

Queer legal theory argues that the law reflects and reinforces dominant social-sexual norms including heterosexuality and gender stereotyping. Queer legal theory examines discourse about legal rights and responsibilities with a critical eye, challenging assumptions about sexual orientation, gender identity, intimacy, and family ties. Queer theorists, for example, have considered how disparate treatment of gay men and lesbians reflects unsupported stereotypes. Queer legal theory has substantial overlap with feminist legal theory as both involve challenging assumptions about gender identity and roles.

* * *

We hope you have enjoyed this romp through American history and jurisprudence. Successful law students—and good lawyers—know a lot more than the narrow details of the law. As you move forward in your legal career, you should keep learning beyond law: read newspapers to keep up with current events and books on subjects that interest you. Be hungry for knowledge; it will give you an edge throughout your career.

CONCLUSION

We hope that reading this book has made you more confident and better prepared for law school. More than that, though, we hope it has excited you about the prospect of becoming a lawyer. You should take pride in your decision to go to law school—you are entering a noble profession. Lawyers are the conscience of our society, using their skills to make society better and more just. They are often leaders in their communities, large and small. Most of the men who wrote the U.S. Constitution were lawyers. As of 2024, twenty-seven of 45 U.S. presidents have been lawyers. More than half of Senators and 30% of House Members are lawyers. Lawyers are mayors and university presidents, cabinet officials and neighborhood association officers, heads of major corporations and owners of small businesses. The large number and wide range of leadership posts filled by attorneys is no surprise. Lawyers are trained to think analytically, communicate effectively, and consider all sides of an issue. The skills and professionalism that you learn in law school will enable you, if you are so inclined, to take the leading role in almost any group of nonlawyers trying to accomplish almost any task. Indeed, "thinking (and communicating) like a lawyer" will become so ingrained that you might occasionally be frustrated in conversations with nonlawyers: they often bring up irrelevancies, contradict themselves, ramble, and generally argue illogically and non-analytically. Be patient with them—you were once like that, too.

We close with a quotation from Oliver Wendell Holmes, who, more than a century ago, was a Harvard law professor and later a U.S. Supreme Court Justice. In 1886, he gave a lecture to Harvard undergraduates who were contemplating a life in the law. In it, he said:

> I say—and I say no longer with any doubt—that a person may live greatly in the law as well as elsewhere; that there as well as elsewhere . . . you may wreak yourself upon life, may drink the bitter cup of heroism, may wear your heart out after the unattainable.[1]

We wish you happiness and success in your pursuit of a life in the law.

1. Oliver Wendell Holmes, Jr., *The Profession of the Law, Conclusion of a Lecture Delivered to Undergraduates of Harvard University* (1886).

ACKNOWLEDGMENTS

Acknowledgments (First Edition)

Many people helped us write this book. Lisa Bressman, Paul Edelman, Jim Ely, Brian Fitzpatrick, John Goldberg, Chris Guthrie, Larry Helfer, Richard Nagareda, Richard K. Neumann, Jr., Jeff Schoenblum, Paige Skiba, Larry Solum, Kevin Stack, Bob Thompson, Ted White, Elizabeth Workman, Henry Young, and Kim Yuracko each read all or part of the manuscript and provided extraordinarily helpful suggestions, sometimes saving us from major errors (you know who you are!). We are grateful for their willingness to share their time and their expertise, often on very short deadlines. Our outstanding research assistant, Andy Lewis (Vanderbilt J.D. 2009), edited our prose, checked our facts, and created prototypes for all the graphics; without him, the book would have been much the poorer. Ben Schrader (Vanderbilt J.D. 2009) provided superb editing suggestions. Our administrative assistant, Linda Reynolds, painstakingly formatted (and reformatted!) the text, polished the graphics, and generally made sure the manuscript was in perfect condition. We also thank the sixteen anonymous colleagues who reviewed either the original outline or the finished manuscript at Aspen's request, adding their ideas. Dean Ed Rubin generously provided financial support and teaching leaves. The library staff and the IT staff at Vanderbilt, under the capable direction of Martin Cerjan and Jason Bradley, responded to our every request with alacrity—and some of our requests were pretty unusual. Carol McGeehan and Steve Errick at Aspen were enthusiastic about the project from the beginning and helped us bring it to fruition. Barbara Roth shepherded us through the publication process, making it easy and painless. Our senior editor, Kaesmene Banks, patiently coordinated all of the technical details. Lisa Wehrle was a wonderful copyeditor. Finally, we thank our past and present students for inspiring us—it is a privilege and a joy to teach generations of future lawyers.

Acknowledgments (Second Edition)

Writing the second edition was a different process from writing the first in many ways. But, in one key respect, it was the same as the first: many people helped us. We are indebted to our colleagues at Vanderbilt who taught from our book and offered invaluable insights on where the first edition worked and where it didn't (and how it could be improved), including Mark Brandon, Brian Fitzpatrick, Daniel Gervais, Terry Maroney, Alistair Newbern, Erin O'Hara O'Connor, Carrie Russell, Amanda Rose, and Jim Rossi. We also learned a great deal from the wonderful J.D. and LL.M. students at Vanderbilt who have read the book and taken the course based on it. Jeff Sheehan (Vanderbilt J.D. 2014) offered thoughtful feedback on the first edition. David Adams (Vanderbilt J.D. 2016) and our assistant Lori Ungurait reviewed the second edition. Finally, Brandy Drinnon, Donna Pavlick, and Todd Morton each helped in different ways to shape the second edition.

Artist Jenny Goldstick is to be credited for creating the infographics that communicate effectively, efficiently, and beautifully a number of the challenging ideas covered in the text. Sue McClung and Casey Pickering at Wolters Kluwer and Carianne King at The Froebe Group guided us through the revision process.

A final thanks to our families. Chris and Paul were patient while we exchanged revisions at odd hours and on weekends. Our children, nieces, and nephews allowed us to use them as characters in our hypotheticals.

We continue to be thankful for the opportunity to introduce new and aspiring law students to the law. Thank you.

Acknowledgments (Third Edition)

In this third edition, we tried to hone and update the book to reflect what we have learned from faculty and students who have used the book in class. We also benefited from excellent suggestions from Charlotte Elam (Vanderbilt J.D. 2020). We are grateful to Justin Billing at Wolters Kluwer and Sue McClung and Georgia Cartmill at The Froebe Group for guiding us through the revision process. We want to express special thanks to Michael Glowacki of Exist Design Studio for creating an outstanding cover to distinguish the third edition. We are grateful to Justin Billing at Wolters Kluwer and Sue McClung and Georgia Cartmill at The Froebe Group for guiding us through the revision process. We want to express special thanks to Michael Glowacki of Exist Design Studio for creating an outstanding cover to distinguish the third edition. We hope you enjoy the result of the work both inside and out of the work both inside and out!

Acknowledgments (Fourth Edition)

We approached revisions for the fourth edition with a genuine appreciation for the continued interest in the book. We are deeply grateful to Whit Stiles for his brilliant editing and to Michael Glowacki for striking graphics. Thanks too to Aaron Cho for his research assistance. Aspen has been a terrific publisher. We feel lucky to have this opportunity to provide you with a refreshed version of the book.

TEST YOUR UNDERSTANDING: ANSWERS AND ANALYSIS

In this section, we offer answers to the "Test Your Understanding" exercises that have simple answers and analyses of those TYU questions that lack a single answer. The answers and analyses are organized by chapter and, within each chapter, by the page on which the TYU appears.

Chapter 1. What to Expect in Law School

Page 22: Types of Knowledge

Direct knowledge: Why you are reading primary sources and what you should get out of them; a preliminary sense of what you should be thinking about when you read and when you are in class; what it means to state or recite a case; that law does not provide certainty; how to be an active participant in your own education; and that making mistakes is inevitable and part of the learning process.

General knowledge: What is in casebooks; how the Socratic method works; and the different meaning s of the term "case."

Available knowledge: First-year courses and the topics they cover.

Examples: The case, statute, and contract illustrating the principle of mitigation; the questions a professor might ask about the mitigation case; and the history of the case method and the Socratic method.

Chapter 2. The Language of the Law

Page 28: Carnival Cruise Line v. Shute

In Contracts class, you are reading the opinion to explore whether the standard form language in the cruise ticket is enforceable against the passenger. In Civil Procedure, you are reading it to explore where the passenger's suit can or should be brought. (We give you further details in the paragraph following the TYU.)

Page 31: Who Won Yates v. United States?

Yates won the case. The excerpt from the case tells you that he was charged with violating §1519. The additional information tells you that §1519 punishes the destruction of "tangible objects," so Yates will lose if a fish is a "tangible object" and will win if it is not. Finally, we quote the Court that, at least as far as §1519 is concerned, "tangible objects" are limited to ("must be") those "used to record or preserve information." You must then use common sense to determine that a fish is *not* a tangible object because it is not used to record or preserve information.

Page 44: Joshua's Fence

FACTS	Joshua builds a fence on what he thinks is his property. Hannah, his neighbor, believes that the fence is on her property. Hannah hires a surveyor, who confirms that it is on her property, but Joshua refuses to take it down.
PROCEDURE	Hannah sues Joshua, seeking an injunction requiring the removal of the fence and damages to compensate Hannah for the cost of hiring the surveyor.
PROCEDURE	The trial court issues the following opinion:
SUBSTANTIVE LAW	If a property owner does not object to another's known trespass on her property, the owner is deemed to have consented to the trespass.
FACTS	Joshua asked Hannah about building the fence, and Hannah did not object.
APPLICATION OF LAW TO FACTS	Therefore, Hannah consented to the fence.
PROCEDURE	Judgment issued in favor of Joshua; no relief is granted to Hannah. Hannah appeals, and the court of appeals affirms (that is, agrees with) the trial court.

Page 46: Deductive Reasoning: Contract Law

This argument is unsound in the same way that "Socrates is a Man (Switched Premise/Conclusion)" is: Just because a valid contract requires consideration and this contract has consideration does *not* mean that this contract is valid. (Just because all men are mortal and Socrates is mortal does not prove that Socrates is a man.) If you switched Premise 2 and the Conclusion it would be sound:

Premise 1: A valid contract requires consideration.
Premise 2: This is a valid contract.
Conclusion: There is consideration for this contract.

Page 48: Deductive Reasoning: Multiple Choice Test

Premise 1: The Law School Admissions Test (LSAT) is a multiple choice test.
Premise 2: All law students took the LSAT before law school.
Conclusion: All law students have taken at least one multiple choice test before law school.

Page 53: Implications of Yates

Your job, as you read, is to identify relevant similarities and differences based on what the court says about both fish (which are not covered by §1519) and the items they suggest would be covered by §1519. That job requires you to think (again, as you read) about what's important to the plurality's decision. Is it that the statute is directed at financial crimes? If so, then #4 and #6 are probably not covered, but the bank robbery version of #5 might be. Is it that the item in question is analogous to a record? If so, then #1 and #4 are easily within §1519, #5 clearly is not, and the others are uncertain. Is it that the item is "falsifiable"? That factor might lead to the inclusion of all of the listed items except possibly #6: you might characterize filing off the serial number as "falsifying" a gun's origins! And under any of these analyses, Snapchat is going to be a difficult case, because it's not clear whether the verbs ("destroy," "conceal," etc.) apply to an item that will be destroyed without any additional action by a person. Needless to say, there are no clear answers to any of these questions. But being able to predict them and analyze them is an important part of reading and being prepared for class.

Chapter 3. The Structure of Government and the Structure of Law

Page 74: Statutory Interpretation: No Vehicles in the Park

1. In order to determine whether bicycles are allowed in the park, you have to interpret the potentially ambiguous term

"vehicles." Does it mean anything with wheels, or anything that is capable of transporting people, or anything that is motorized? There is no clear answer to the question whether the prohibition includes bicycles or any of the other items listed.

You have to make arguments about the breadth of the meaning of the term "vehicles." Arguments you might make include quoting dictionary definitions, identifying the most common usage of the term, comparing the item in question to something that the rule clearly intends to include as a vehicle (a car), looking at the likely purpose of the law, asking how the term "vehicles" is defined in other laws, and asking about the likely consequences of interpreting "vehicles" to include or exclude each of the listed items. You must distinguish between plausible or arguable interpretations (an electric scooter and a horse-drawn carriage *might or might not* be vehicles) and implausible interpretations (a wheelchair is *probably not* a vehicle).

2. The tank examples ask you to continue the same analysis, ranging from easy examples (a statue of a tank almost certainly is not a vehicle, and a fully functional tank almost certainly is a vehicle) to very hard ones. Again, you will want to ask why the city banned vehicles from the park, and what might follow from deciding that each of the listed items is or is not a vehicle.

Page 79: Statutory Interpretation: No Vehicles in the Park—Follow Up

This exercise gives you more information about the legislative purpose of the "no vehicles" statute discussed above and also about other statutes that might offer relevant information for interpreting the "no vehicles" statute.

1. The information on legislative purpose could support contradictory conclusions because the council members supported the same outcome for very different and possibly conflicting reasons. Like cars, bicycles might be dangerous to small children; bicycles also might interfere with the rest and relaxation of other park users. Thus, the council members who focused on safety and those who focused on quiet might agree that bicycles fall within their purpose. (You could argue, though, that quiet bicycles don't interfere with relaxation.) But the

environmentally conscious council members probably did not want to ban bicycles when they supported the statute; indeed, they probably would have wanted to encourage the use of bicycles. While the legislative background has helped to inform and focus our interpretation of the statute (we have confirmation that cars were clearly intended to be covered), it does not lead us to a clear answer on whether the statute prohibits bicycles. You will still have to compare bicycles to known vehicles (cars) on the three relevant criteria: safety, disruption of relaxation, and environmental impact.

2. Ordinary tools of statutory interpretation would at first suggest that if "vehicles" in the "emergency" statute covers both cars and bicycles, then "vehicles" in the "park" statute should be interpreted the same way. But you can distinguish the two statutes by their purposes and by how the inclusion of bicycles serves those purposes. In the "emergency" statute, including bicycles serves the purpose of clearing the road so that the emergency vehicle can proceed as quickly as possible. In the "park" statute, including bicycles, as we have seen, does not serve the purpose of environmental protection, and serves the other two purposes somewhat weakly. Again, there is no right answer.

Chapter 4. The Structure of the American Legal System

Page 91: Where to Appeal

If you lose a case in the U.S. District Court for the Southern District of Florida, you must file your appeal in the U.S. Court of Appeals for the Eleventh Circuit. As reflected in the federal circuit map (page 90), the Eleventh Circuit includes Alabama, Florida, and Georgia. Prior to October 1, 1981, those states were included with Louisiana, Mississippi, and Texas in the Fifth Circuit. Thus, if you are reading a decision before that date, an appeal from the Southern District of Florida would have been heard by the old Fifth Circuit. Congress divided the Fifth Circuit into two circuits, creating the Eleventh Circuit when the court's caseload became too large for a single court. Since 1981, appeals from district courts in Louisiana, Mississippi, and Texas have been heard by the Fifth Circuit, and appeals from district courts in Alabama, Florida, and Georgia have been heard by the Eleventh Circuit.

Page 95: Binding Precedent

A New York supreme court is a trial court in the New York state judicial system, as reflected in the judicial hierarchy graphic (page 87). It must follow the decisions of the New York Appellate Division, which is the intermediate appellate court in New York, and the New York Court of Appeals, which is the court of last resort. If opinions of the New York Appellate Division and New York Court of Appeals appear to disagree, the New York Court of Appeals opinion controls. If a New York supreme court is deciding a question controlled by federal law, then it must follow precedent from the U.S. Supreme Court.

The Tennessee Supreme Court is the highest state court in Tennessee. It is the final word on questions of Tennessee state law. On questions of federal law, it must follow the decisions of the U.S. Supreme Court.

The U.S. District Court for the Eastern District of California is a trial court in the federal judicial system. It must follow the precedents from the U.S. Court of Appeals for the Ninth Circuit (as the federal circuit map on page 90 shows, California is in the Ninth Circuit) and from the U.S. Supreme Court.

The U.S. Court of Appeals for the Second Circuit is an intermediate appellate court in the federal judicial system. It must follow precedents from the U.S. Supreme Court.

Chapter 5. Fundamental Legal Concepts

Page 105: Rules and Standards: Contract Law Rules

These three contract law examples reflect different affirmative defenses to the enforcement of a contract. If a defendant successfully asserts the defense, then the plaintiff cannot enforce the contract.

A valid contract between two parties will be enforced unless it is against public policy. Of the three laws, this one grants the greatest discretion to the decision maker and is therefore the most standard-like. A determination of what is "public policy" requires a judgment call and whether a particular contract is "against" public policy will likewise require weighing case-specific circumstances.

A contract that cannot be completed within a year will not be enforced unless it is in writing. This law (the Statute of Frauds one-year provision) lies somewhere on the continuum between rule and standard. On the one hand, the law leaves no discretion as to the length of time at which a writing is required (one year). But, on the other hand, it grants some discretion in determining whether a contract *can* be completed within that period. It directs the court to consider whether it would be possible for it to be completed within one year. Thus, it leaves to the judge the discretion to evaluate what is reasonably possible in light of the parties' intentions and the circumstances of the agreement.

A **contract is not enforceable against a person under 18 years of age.** This is the most rule-like of the three examples. The law operates automatically once the predicate facts—whether the person is under 18 years of age—are determined. The law leaves no room for discretion in its application because chronological age is a mechanical question. If a person is under 18 years of age, then the contract cannot be enforced.

Page 108: Rules and Standards: Attendance Policy

1. The simplest rule to meet those guidelines would be something like the following: "An absence will result in a grade decrease of one-third of a letter (from an A- to a B+, for example) in a student's final course grade." The rule is clear, predictable, and easy to apply.
2. Ben would not suffer any consequences under this rule because he is not, as a technical matter, absent from class. Thus, the attendance rule seems underinclusive because it does not punish a student who *effectively* misses class and treats Ben like a student who attends the entire class every day.
3. Although Jonathan's absence is legitimate, a clear rule will treat him the same as a student who misses class without a good reason. The professor likely would want to discourage students with contagious illnesses from attending classes, but the clear rule does not consider the reason for a student's absence. Thus, the rule is overinclusive because it punishes a student who has a good reason for avoiding other people and thus missing class. It seems unfair that the rule punishes Jonathan but not Ben.
4. You could add exceptions to your rule to change the outcome in both cases. You could expand the rule to cover absences and tardiness. And you could make an exception for absences

due to contagious illnesses. Thus, your new policy would be this: "An absence or tardiness not due to a contagious illness will result in a grade decrease of one-third of a letter in a student's final course grade."

5. Under the revised policy, Elizabeth and Sarah will each suffer a grade decrease. If that seems unfair to Elizabeth because a car accident, like a contagious illness, seems like a good reason for missing class, then you could add car accidents to the list. But what other events would you also have to anticipate and add? If it also seems unfair that Sarah is being treated like students who miss most or all of class, then you could set a cutoff time (late more than 10 minutes, 15 minutes, half of the class?). Such a rule would create an incentive for students to attend class even if they will be late. As the list of exceptions and clarifications grow, however, the professor will have to figure out how and why to add other excuses or clarifications.
6. One possible policy would be this: "Unavoidable absences are excused, but substantial tardiness is not." But as soon as you insert "unavoidable" or "substantial," you leave the professor discretion to determine which absences are truly unavoidable and which are not, and how much tardiness is substantial and how much is not. A rule has the advantage of giving students sufficient notice of the consequences of their actions (if they don't leave enough time to get to class, then their grade will be lowered). But it leads to results that appear inequitable and, in fact, counter to the professor's stated goals.

Page 110: Categorization and Balancing Tests: Driveway Items

A categorization test might provide for two categories which must both be satisfied for homeowner liability: dangerousness and unusualness. "If a homeowner leaves in her driveway a dangerous item not typically stored there, then the homeowner is liable for any damage caused by the item. If the item is not dangerous or is typically stored in the driveway, then the homeowner is not liable."

A balancing test could require the court to weigh the relative risk posed by the item against the need for a homeowner to be able to store it in her driveway. "A homeowner will be liable for the damage caused by items left in her driveway if the risks posed by the item outweigh the ordinary value of keeping the item in the driveway."

Page 114: States of Mind

Intentional:	Subjective, rule
Knowing:	Subjective, between rule and standard ("almost certainly" gives some discretion)
Reckless:	Subjective, standard
Negligent:	Objective, standard
Strict:	Objective, rule

Page 116: Interpreting Precedent: Carrying a Gun

To argue that keeping a gun in the trunk *is* carrying it, you would note the similarities between the glove compartment and the trunk. In neither case is the gun actually in the hands of the person committing the felony; in both cases the person would have to open a part of the car to get to the gun; and in neither case is the gun visible to other participants in the drug deal. You would want to make arguments (and hope to see reasoning in the case that supports them) that the purpose of the statute is to deter people from taking guns with them when they commit felonies, and thus that it does not matter where the gun is in the vehicle. To argue that keeping a gun in the trunk *is not* carrying it, you would note the differences between the glove compartment and the trunk. The glove compartment, but not the trunk, is inside the vehicle (as is the drug dealer), and thus more accessible to occupants of the car than the trunk is. You would want to make arguments (and hope to see reasoning in the case that supports them) that the purpose of the statute is to prevent felonies from exploding into gun violence, and thus that only easily accessible guns are within the statutory language.

Page 117-18: Burdens of Proof

The court should affirm the judgment. If the jury concluded that the plaintiff proved the crucial fact by clear and convincing evidence, it necessarily also concluded that the plaintiff proved the fact by a preponderance of the evidence. The clear-and-convincing standard is *harder* to satisfy than the preponderance standard—it requires more evidence and more certainty. The error is therefore harmless because the jury would have had an even easier time finding for the plaintiff under the correct (preponderance) standard.

Page 121: Standards of Review: Joshua's Fence Redux

The appellate court should apply the appropriate standard of law given the nature of the trial court's decision—it is a legal holding or a factual one? Let's consider each example:

> **"If a property owner does not object to another's known trespass on her property, the owner is deemed to have consented to the trespass."** This is a statement of law, and the appellate court should review it de novo.
>
> **"Joshua asked Hannah about building the fence, and Hannah did not object."** This is a finding of fact, and the appellate court should reverse it only if it is clearly erroneous.
>
> **"Therefore, Hannah consented to the fence."** This is an application of the law to the facts. Assuming that it is a correct statement of law, the appellate court should reverse the holding only if it is clearly erroneous.

Page 124: Speed Limits

The benefits of higher speed limits include: gains in efficiency as people arrive at their destinations sooner, reductions in frustration as people drive whatever is comfortable, and reductions in enforcement costs as fewer people exceed the limits. The costs of higher speed limits include: increased accidents (and therefore probably increased deaths, injuries, and property damage) and increased pollution. Abandoning speed limits would have the same benefits and costs—to a greater extent than simply raising them—and would also have one additional benefit: because speed limits are difficult to enforce and are in fact often not enforced, many people speed (if only a little). The cavalier attitude toward obeying speed limits might incline people against obeying the law at all and might undermine other laws. Abandoning speed limits altogether would eliminate this cost.

Page 125: Expected Value: Lottery Game

In order to evaluate whether to play this game, we have to calculate the expected value of playing, which is equal to the expected benefit less the expected cost for each possible outcome. The expected benefit from playing the game is the payoff from winning ($50) multiplied by the probability of winning *plus* the payoff from losing ($0) multiplied by the probability of losing. The expected cost is the same whether we win or lose: $10.

> The expected value of the game with a 10 percent probability of winning is: [($50 × .10) + ($0 × .90)] – $10 =$5 – $10 = – $5. The expected value is a $5 loss.
>
> The expected value of the game with a 50 percent probability of winning is: [($50 × .50) + ($0 × .50)]–$10 = $25 – $10 = $15. The expected value is a $15 gain.

Thus, you should play if the probability of winning is 50 percent but not if it is 10 percent. Can you figure out at what probability the game switches from one with a negative expected value to a positive expected value (from a losing game to a winning one)? The answer turns on the cost compared to the payout. If the cost is less than the payout multiplied by the probability of winning, then it is a winning game. To make that determination, ask "what percentage of $50 is $10?" The answer is 20 percent. If the probability of winning is 20 percent, then the expected value is zero (the cost equals the expected benefit). If the probability is greater than 20 percent, you should play.

Page 131: Cognitive Bias: Slip and Fall

1. Danny has committed at least one type of decision-making error: anchoring. He has allowed the multimillion-dollar award to anchor his expectation about the value of his claim. While this award also came in a slip-and-fall case, Sasha knows from reading other cases that the two cases are obviously quite different (or the multimillion-dollar award is highly unusual). Danny may also be suffering from self-serving (or egocentric) bias, imagining that his case must be as strong and valuable as the one that led to a multimillion-dollar award.
2. Sasha can seek to overcome both of those biases in the same way: She should compile data on cases similar to Danny's and present those cases to Danny for his consideration. As Danny has more information, he will be able to revise his estimate in light of the new data.

INDEX

M

N